POOL MAINTENANCE 101

A Beginners DIY Guide On Removing Algae,
Understanding Water Chemistry, & Looking After Your
Pool!

JASON BROWN

Contents

1. Introduction

Welcome to the exciting world of pool maintenance! Whether you're a proud new pool owner or a seasoned veteran looking to improve your skills, this comprehensive guide will provide you with the knowledge and tools necessary to keep your pool in pristine condition. In this chapter, we will introduce you to the basics of pool maintenance and set the stage for more detailed information in subsequent chapters.

Many people dream of owning a swimming pool, providing endless hours of fun, relaxation, and entertainment. However, with great pleasure comes great responsibility. Proper pool maintenance is essential to ensure the health and safety of those who use it and prolong the life of your pool and its equipment. By learning about pool care and establishing a consistent maintenance routine, you can enjoy the benefits of your pool without the stress of unexpected issues or costly repairs.

At first glance, pool maintenance may seem like a daunting task. There are chemicals to balance, equipment to maintain, and a seemingly endless list of tasks to perform. However, with a bit of patience and proper guidance, you will soon find that maintaining your pool is manageable and enjoyable. After all, there is something deeply satisfying about knowing that your pool is clean, safe, and ready for use whenever you or your loved ones wish to take a dip.

This book will cover the essential aspects of pool maintenance, from understanding the importance of regular pool care to mastering the basic tasks and techniques required to keep your pool in top shape. We will also delve into the world of pool water chemistry, providing tips and tricks to maintain the perfect balance of chemicals in your pool. By the end of this book, you will have the knowledge and confidence to tackle pool maintenance like a pro.

As you embark on this journey, remember that pool maintenance is not a one-size-fits-all endeavor. Each pool is unique, with its own variables that may require a slightly different approach. However, the fundamental principles of pool care remain the same, and by understanding these principles, you can adapt your maintenance routine to suit your pool's specific needs.

With some time and effort, you will soon be on your way to enjoying a crystal-clear, sparkling pool that is the envy of your neighbors and the delight of your family and friends.

Understanding the Importance of Regular Pool Care

A shimmering, crystal-clear pool epitomizes relaxation and enjoyment on a hot summer day. However, achieving and maintaining that pristine condition requires consistent care and attention. This chapter will delve into the importance of regular pool care, how it can save you time and money and ensure a safe and enjoyable swimming experience for you and your loved ones.

First and foremost, regular pool care is essential for ensuring the health and safety of swimmers. A well-maintained pool prevents the growth of harmful bacteria, algae, and other microorganisms that can cause skin irritations, eye infections, and even more severe health issues. By consistently monitoring and adjusting your pool's water chemistry, you can keep these potential hazards at bay and provide a safe environment for everyone to enjoy.

In addition to safeguarding the health of swimmers, regular pool care also plays a crucial role in preserving the longevity of your pool and its equipment. Neglecting pool maintenance can lead to the buildup of debris, dirt, and other contaminants, which can clog filters, strain pumps, and damage other essential components. This can result in costly repairs or even the need for complete equipment replacement. By investing time and effort into routine pool care, you can prevent these issues and extend the lifespan of your pool and its components.

Another key benefit of regular pool care is preventing unsightly and stubborn problems such as algae blooms and staining. Algae, in particular, can be challenging to eliminate once it has taken hold, often requiring extensive scrubbing, shocking, and even draining of the pool. By maintaining a consistent cleaning schedule and properly balancing your pool's water chemistry, you can prevent these issues from arising in the first place, saving you time, effort, and frustration.

Lastly, regular pool care contributes to the overall aesthetic appeal of your outdoor space. A well-maintained pool is an inviting and attractive centerpiece for your backyard, perfect for hosting gatherings with friends and family or simply enjoying a peaceful afternoon swim. On the other hand, a neglected pool can quickly become an eyesore, detracting from the beauty and value of your property.

In conclusion, understanding the importance of regular pool care is the first step toward maintaining a safe, functional, and visually appealing swimming environment. By investing time and effort into routine maintenance tasks, you can protect the health of swimmers, extend the life of your pool and its equipment, and ensure that your backyard oasis remains a source of relaxation and enjoyment for years to come. In the following chapters, we will explore the essential tools, equipment, and techniques required for effective pool maintenance and tips for maintaining optimal water chemistry and establishing a consistent pool care routine.

2. Different types of pools

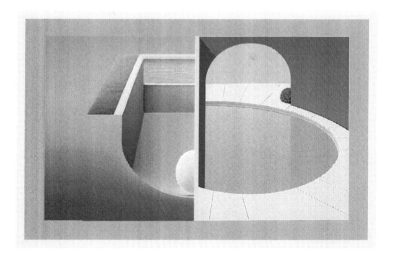

Saltwater vs Chlorine pools

Two of the most popular types of swimming pools are chlorine pools and salt water pools. In this chapter, we will explore the differences between these two types of pools, including the benefits and drawbacks of each.

Chlorine Pools

Chlorine pools are the most common type of swimming pool in the world. This is largely due to the fact that they are relatively inexpensive and easy to maintain. In a chlorine pool, chlorine is added to the water to sanitize it and prevent the growth of harmful bacteria and algae. Chlorine can be added to the water in a number of ways, including liquid or granular chlorine, chlorine tablets, or a salt chlorinator. Regardless of the method used, it is important to maintain the appropriate level of chlorine in the water to ensure that the pool is safe to swim in.

Benefits of Chlorine Pools:

- Chlorine is a powerful sanitizer that can kill harmful bacteria and algae.

- Chlorine is relatively inexpensive and easy to obtain.

- Chlorine can be added to the water in a variety of ways, giving pool owners flexibility and convenience.

- Chlorine pools are generally less expensive to install than salt water pools.

Drawbacks of Chlorine Pools:

- Chlorine can cause skin and eye irritation in some individuals.

- Chlorine can be harmful to the environment if not properly disposed of.

- Chlorine pools require regular maintenance to ensure that the appropriate level of chlorine is maintained in the water.

Salt Water Pools

Salt water pools are becoming increasingly popular, particularly among those who are looking for a more natural and eco-friendly swimming experience. In a salt water pool, a salt cell generator is used to convert salt in the water into chlorine. The salt cell generator uses electrolysis to break down the salt molecules and create chlorine gas, which is then dissolved into the water. The process is continuous and creates a consistent level of chlorine in the water.

Benefits of Salt Water Pools:

- Salt water pools have lower levels of chlorine than traditional chlorine pools, making them less harsh on the skin and eyes.

- Salt water pools have a more natural and pleasant taste than chlorine pools.

- Salt water pools require less maintenance than chlorine pools, as the salt cell generator creates a consistent level of chlorine in the water.

- Salt water pools are more eco-friendly, as they do not require the constant addition of chlorine to the water.

Drawbacks of Salt Water Pools:

- Salt water pools require a larger initial investment, as a salt cell generator is required.

- Salt water pools require more maintenance to keep the salt cell generator clean and functioning properly.

- Salt water pools may require the addition of chemicals other than chlorine to maintain the appropriate levels of pH and alkalinity in the water.

- Salt water pools may be more difficult to maintain in areas with hard water, as the salt can build up in the pool over time.

In conclusion, both chlorine pools and salt water pools have their advantages and disadvantages. Ultimately, the choice between the two will depend on a number of factors, including personal preference, budget, and maintenance requirements. Before making a decision, it is important to do your research and consult with a pool professional to determine which type of pool is right for your needs.

. . .

Finding the total water volume of your swimming pool

Knowing the volume of your pool is important for several reasons:

1. Proper Chemical Dosing

To keep your pool clean and safe for swimming, you need to maintain the proper chemical balance in the water. The amount of chemicals you need to add to your pool will depend on its volume. If you don't know the volume of your pool, you may end up adding too little or too much chemicals, which can lead to imbalanced water chemistry and potential health hazards for swimmers.

2. Proper Filtration

The size of your pool's filter, pump, and other equipment should be properly sized to handle the volume of your pool. If you don't know the volume of your pool, you may not have the right equipment to properly filter and circulate the water. This can lead to poor water quality, algae growth, and other problems.

3. Maintenance and Repairs

Knowing the volume of your pool can help you estimate the amount of water needed to be replaced during maintenance or repairs. It can also help you estimate the amount of cleaning chemicals needed for regular maintenance.

4. Compliance with Local Regulations

In some areas, there are regulations that require pool owners to maintain a certain volume of water in their pool. Knowing the volume of your pool can help you ensure that you are complying with these regulations.

. . .

Calculating the volume of your pool

You will need to measure the dimensions of your pool and use a formula based on those measurements. The formula you use will depend on the shape of your pool.

Here are the formulas for calculating the volume of some common pool shapes:

Rectangular or Square Pools

Volume = length x width x average depth x 7.5. For example, if your pool is 20 feet long, 10 feet wide, and has an average depth of 5 feet, the formula would be: 20 x 10 x 5 x 7.5 = 7,500 gallons.

Circular Pools

Volume = 3.14 x radius x radius x average depth x 7.5. For example, if your pool has a radius of 10 feet and an average depth of 5 feet, the formula would be: 3.14 x 10 x 10 x 5 x 7.5 = 11,775 gallons.

Oval Pools

Volume = length x width x average depth x 5.9. For example, if your pool is 25 feet long, 15 feet wide, and has an average depth of 4 feet, the formula would be: 25 x 15 x 4 x 5.9 = 8,850 gallons.

You can use a measuring tape or a long rope to measure the length and width of your pool, and a pool depth marker or a long pole with a weight attached to measure the average depth. If you are still unsure about how to measure your pool or calculate its volume, you can scan this QR code that will take you to an online calculator.

Chapter 2 Summary

1. Chlorine pools are the most common type of pool as they are inexpensive and easy to maintain. Chlorine is added to the water in various forms to sanitize and prevent bacterial growth.

2. Saltwater pools are increasingly popular for a more natural and eco-friendly swimming experience. Salt cells are used to convert salt into chlorine gas, which is then dissolved into the water to maintain a consistent level of chlorine.

3. Chlorine pools have high levels of chlorine and require regular maintenance, while saltwater pools are less harsh on skin and eyes, require less maintenance, and are more eco-friendly.

4. The choice between chlorine and saltwater pools will depend on personal preference, budget, and maintenance requirements.

5. Knowing the volume of your pool is important for proper chemical dosing, filtration, maintenance, and repairs, and compliance with local regulations.

6. To calculate the volume of your pool, you need to measure the dimensions of your pool and use a formula based on its shape.

3. Pool Cleaning Equipment and Tools

A sparkling clean pool epitomizes a perfect summer day, inviting you to dive in and enjoy its refreshing embrace. However, maintaining that crystal-clear water and pristine pool environment requires consistent care and attention. As a pool owner, it is essential to understand the importance of pool cleaning equipment and tools to ensure a safe and enjoyable swimming experience for you and your guests.

In this chapter, we will explore the various types of pool cleaning equipment and tools available in the market, ranging from essential items every pool owner should have to advanced tools to make pool maintenance more efficient. We will also discuss how to choose the right equipment for your pool type and size and the proper care and storage of these tools to prolong their lifespan and effectiveness. By the end of this chapter, you will understand the importance of investing in quality pool cleaning equipment and tools and how they can make your pool maintenance journey a breeze.

Whether you are a new pool owner or an experienced one looking to upgrade your pool cleaning arsenal, this chapter will provide valuable insights and recommendations to help you make informed decisions. So, let's dive in and explore the fascinating world of pool cleaning equipment and tools!

Essential Pool Cleaning Equipment for Every Pool Owner

As a pool owner, you understand the importance of keeping your pool clean, safe, and well-maintained. A sparkling pool looks inviting and ensures a healthy swimming environment for you and your family. To achieve this, you must have the right pool cleaning equipment. This section will discuss the essential pool cleaning tools that every pool owner should have in their arsenal.

Skimmer Net

A skimmer net is a simple yet indispensable tool for any pool owner. It comprises a long pole with a fine mesh net attached to the end. Skimmer nets are perfect for removing leaves, insects, and other debris floating on the water's surface. Regular skimming helps maintain the cleanliness of your pool and reduces the workload on your pool's filtration system.

Pool Brush

A pool brush is another essential tool for keeping your pool clean. It is designed to scrub your pool's walls, floor, and steps, removing algae, dirt, and grime that can accumulate over time. Pool brushes come in various sizes and materials, such as nylon, stainless steel, or a combination of both, to cater to different pool surfaces. Regular brushing prevents algae buildup and keeps your pool looking pristine.

Vacuum Head and Hose

A vacuum head and hose are crucial for removing debris and dirt settled at the bottom of your pool. The vacuum head attaches to a telescopic pole and is connected to the pool's skimmer or suction port through a hose. Moving the vacuum head along the pool floor sucks up debris, which is then trapped in the pool's filtration system. Regular vacuuming helps maintain water clarity and reduces the need for chemical treatments.

Water Test Kit

Maintaining the correct water chemistry is vital for a healthy and safe swimming environment. A water test kit allows you to check the chlorine levels, pH, alkalinity, and other essential parameters in your pool water. Regular testing helps you adjust your pool's chemical balance, ensuring the water remains clean and safe for swimming.

Pool Shock

Pool shock is a concentrated form of chlorine that eliminates bacteria, algae, and other contaminants from your pool water. Shocking your pool regularly, especially after heavy use or a rainstorm, helps maintain water quality and prevents the growth of harmful microorganisms.

Telescopic Pole

A telescopic pole is a versatile and essential tool that can be extended to various lengths and is used with other cleaning tools, such as skimmer nets, pool brushes, and vacuum heads. A telescopic pole allows you to reach all pool areas, ensuring thorough cleaning and maintenance.

Investing in these essential pool cleaning tools will make your pool maintenance routine more efficient and effective. Regularly using these tools can keep your pool in top condition and enjoy a clean, safe, and inviting swimming environment. The following section will explore advanced tools that can further enhance your pool maintenance efforts.

Advanced Tools for Efficient Pool Maintenance

As a pool owner, you may already be familiar with the essential pool cleaning equipment such as skimmers, brushes, and vacuum cleaners. However, it's worth considering investing in some advanced tools to make your pool maintenance routine more efficient and effective. These tools save you time and effort and ensure that your pool remains in pristine condition all year round. This section will explore some of the advanced tools that can elevate your pool maintenance game to the next level.

Robotic Pool Cleaners

These state-of-the-art devices are designed to automate pool cleaning, making it a breeze for pool owners. Robotic pool cleaners have advanced features such as intelligent navigation, programmable cleaning cycles, and powerful suction capabilities. They can efficiently remove dirt, debris, and algae from your pool's floor, walls, and waterline. Although they come with a higher price tag, the convenience and time-saving benefits they offer make them a worthwhile investment.

Automatic Pool Covers

An automatic pool cover is a fantastic addition to any pool maintenance toolkit. Not only does it provide safety and help reduce evaporation, but it also keeps debris out of your pool. By preventing leaves, dirt, and other contaminants from entering the pool, an automatic pool cover significantly reduces the required cleaning. This means less time spent on pool maintenance and more time enjoying your pool.

Digital Water Test Kits

Maintaining the proper chemical balance in your pool ensures a safe and healthy swimming environment. Digital water test kits offer a more accurate and convenient way to test your pool's water chemistry than traditional test strips or liquid test kits. These advanced tools provide precise readings of pH, chlorine, and other essential chemical levels, allowing you to make informed decisions about your pool's chemical treatment.

Salt Chlorine Generators

If you want an eco-friendly and cost-effective alternative to traditional chlorine-based pool sanitization, consider investing in a salt chlorine generator. These devices convert salt into chlorine, providing continuous sanitization without the need for frequent chemical additions. In addition to reducing the time and effort spent on pool maintenance, salt chlorine generators offer a more comfortable swimming experience, as the water feels softer and less irritating to the skin and eyes.

Pool Skimmer Systems

Upgrading your pool's skimmer system can significantly improve its efficiency in removing debris from the water's surface. Advanced skimmer systems are designed to enhance water circulation, which helps to keep your pool cleaner and reduces the workload on your filtration system. Some models even come with built-in leaf canisters, making it easier to dispose of collected debris.

In conclusion, investing in advanced pool maintenance tools can significantly improve the efficiency and effectiveness of your pool care routine. While some of these tools may require a larger upfront investment, the time and effort saved in the long run make them a worthwhile addition to any pool owner's toolkit. By choosing the right advanced tools for your pool type and size, you can ensure that your pool remains clean, safe, and enjoyable for years.

Choosing the Right Equipment for Your Pool Type and Size

The appropriate pool cleaning equipment and tools are crucial for maintaining a pristine and inviting swimming environment. The type and size of your pool are two key factors that should be considered when making these decisions. In this section, we will guide you through choosing the right equipment for your specific pool type and size, ensuring that you invest in the most effective and efficient tools for your needs.

First, let's discuss the different types of pools. There are three main categories: above-ground, in-ground, and semi-in-ground pools. Each type has its unique characteristics and requirements for cleaning and maintenance.

Above-ground pools are typically smaller and more affordable than their in-ground counterparts. They are also easier to clean, as they often have less surface area to cover. A simple manual pool vacuum, skimmer, and brush should suffice for most cleaning tasks for these pools. However, if your above-ground pool is larger, consider investing in an automatic pool cleaner to save time and energy.

In-ground pools come in various shapes and sizes, often requiring more advanced equipment to keep them clean. For these pools, an automatic pool cleaner is highly recommended. There are several types of automatic cleaners, such as suction-side, pressure-side, and robotic cleaners. Each has its own advantages and disadvantages, so it's essential to research and choose the one that best suits your pool's specific needs.

Semi-in-ground pools combine elements of both above-ground and in-ground pools. They are partially submerged in the ground, making them more challenging to clean than above-ground pools but less so than in-ground pools. A combination of manual and automatic cleaning tools may be the most effective for these pools.

Now that we've discussed the different pool types let's consider the size of your pool. The larger your pool, the more time and effort it will take to clean it. Therefore, investing in advanced cleaning tools and equipment is especially important for larger pools. For example, a telescopic pole with interchangeable heads for skimming, brushing, and vacuuming can make cleaning a large pool much more manageable. A high-capacity pool filter and a powerful pool pump will also help maintain water quality and circulation in larger pools.

Choosing the right pool cleaning equipment and tools for your pool type and size is essential for efficient and effective maintenance. By considering the unique characteristics of your pool and investing in the appropriate tools, you can ensure that your swimming environment remains clean, safe, and enjoyable for years to come.

Proper Care and Storage of Pool Cleaning Tools

Just as important as having the right pool cleaning equipment and tools is taking proper care of them. By maintaining your tools and storing them correctly, you can extend their lifespan and ensure they remain effective in keeping your pool clean and well-maintained. This section will discuss the best practices for caring for and storing your pool cleaning tools.

First and foremost, cleaning your tools after each use is crucial. This may seem a no-brainer, but many pool owners must pay more attention to this simple yet essential step. By rinsing your tools with fresh water, you can remove any chemicals, dirt, and debris that may have accumulated during the cleaning process. This prevents the buildup of grime and corrosion, which can damage your tools over time.

When it comes to brushes and vacuum heads, inspect the bristles and attachments for any signs of wear or damage. Replace any worn-out parts as needed to maintain the effectiveness of your tools. Additionally, it's a good idea to periodically lubricate any moving parts on your equipment, such as the wheels on your vacuum head or the hinges on your skimmer net, to ensure smooth operation.

Proper storage is another key aspect of caring for your pool cleaning tools. Ideally, you should store your equipment in a cool, dry place, away from direct sunlight and harsh weather conditions. Exposure to the elements can cause your tools to deteriorate more quickly, so investing in a storage shed or a designated area in your garage is a wise decision.

When storing your tools, hanging them up rather than placing them on the ground is best. This not only keeps your tools organized and easy to access but also prevents them from coming into contact with moisture, dirt, and pests that can cause damage. For items like telescopic poles and hoses, coil them neatly to prevent kinks and tangles that can weaken the material over time.

Lastly, conducting regular inspections of your pool cleaning equipment and tools is important. Check for any signs of wear, damage, or corrosion, and address any issues promptly. By staying on top of maintenance and storage, you can ensure that your tools remain in optimal condition, allowing you to keep your pool clean and well-maintained effortlessly.

Investing in quality pool cleaning equipment and tools is only half the battle. Proper care and storage are essential in prolonging the life of your tools and ensuring their effectiveness in maintaining your pool. Following the best practices outlined in this section, you can keep your tools in top shape and enjoy a clean, sparkling pool for years.

Investing in Quality Pool Cleaning Equipment and Tools

In conclusion, maintaining a clean and healthy swimming pool is a crucial responsibility for every pool owner. As we have explored throughout this chapter, investing in quality pool-cleaning equipment and tools is vital to this process. Equipping yourself with the right tools ensures that your pool remains a safe, enjoyable, and inviting space for family and friends.

We have discussed the essential pool cleaning equipment that every pool owner should have, such as a pool skimmer, vacuum, and brush. These essential tools are indispensable for protecting your pool from debris, dirt, and algae. We have also delved into advanced tools for the efficient pool maintenance, such as robotic pool cleaners and automatic chemical dispensers, which can save you time and effort while thoroughly cleaning.

Choosing the right equipment for your pool type and size is also crucial, as different pools have unique requirements and challenges. By carefully considering factors such as your pool's shape, size, and surface material, you can select the most appropriate tools to maintain your pool effectively.

Proper care and storage of your pool cleaning tools are essential to prolong their lifespan and ensure their effectiveness. By cleaning, drying, and storing your equipment correctly, you can protect your investment and avoid the need for frequent replacements.

Ultimately, investing in quality pool cleaning equipment and tools is an investment in the health and enjoyment of your swimming pool. By prioritizing the cleanliness and maintenance of your pool, you can provide a safe and enjoyable environment for all who use it for years to come.

Chapter 3 Summary

1. Maintaining a clean and healthy swimming pool is essential for every pool owner, and investing in quality pool cleaning equipment and tools is crucial for achieving this goal.

2. Essential pool cleaning tools include a skimmer net, pool brush, vacuum head, hose, water test kit, pool shock, and a telescopic pole. These tools help remove debris, dirt, and algae and maintain proper water chemistry.

3. Advanced pool maintenance tools, such as robotic pool cleaners, automatic pool covers, digital water test kits, salt chlorine generators, and advanced skimmer systems, can save time and effort while providing a thorough cleaning.

4. Choosing the right equipment for your pool type (above-ground, in-ground, or semi-in-ground) and size is crucial, as different pools have unique requirements and challenges.

5. Proper care and storage of pool cleaning tools are essential to prolong their lifespan and ensure their effectiveness. This includes cleaning and drying tools after each use, inspecting for wear and damage, and storing them in a cool, dry place away from direct sunlight and harsh weather conditions.

6. Regular inspections of your pool cleaning equipment and tools help identify signs of wear, damage, or corrosion, allowing you to address any issues promptly and maintain the effectiveness of your tools.

7. Investing in quality pool cleaning equipment and tools is an investment in the health and enjoyment of your swimming pool, providing a safe and enjoyable environment for all who use it.

8. By prioritizing the cleanliness and maintenance of your pool and equipping yourself with the right tools, you can

enjoy the benefits of a well-maintained pool for years to come.

4. Skimming, Brushing, and Vacuuming Techniques

In this chapter we'll dive into the essential techniques that will transform your pool maintenance routine and elevate the cleanliness of your swimming pool to new heights. Skimming, brushing, and vacuuming are the trifecta of pool care, each vital in maintaining a pristine and inviting aquatic oasis. In this chapter, we will explore the ins and outs of these techniques, equipping you with the knowledge and skills to master the art of pool maintenance.

Imagine a sparkling clean pool, free from debris, algae, and dirt, with crystal-clear water that beckons you to dive in and enjoy its refreshing embrace. This vision can become a reality by properly applying skimming, brushing, and vacuuming techniques. These methods work harmoniously to ensure that your pool remains in tip-top shape, providing a safe and enjoyable environment for you, your family, and your guests.

In the following sections, we will delve into the specifics of each technique, starting with mastering the art of pool skimming. We will then move on to effective brushing techniques for a clean pool surface, followed by tips and tricks for optimal vacuuming results. Finally, we will discuss how to balance these three techniques in your pool maintenance routine.

By the end of this chapter, you will have a comprehensive understanding of skimming, brushing, and vacuuming techniques, enabling you to achieve a sparkling clean pool that is visually appealing but also safe and hygienic. So, let's dive in and begin our journey toward mastering the art of pool maintenance!

Mastering the Art of Pool Skimming

Pool skimming is essential to maintaining a clean and healthy swimming environment. This simple yet effective technique helps remove debris, such as leaves, insects, and dirt, from the water's surface before it can sink to the bottom. This section will explore the art of skimming, providing valuable tips and insights to ensure your pool remains pristine and inviting.

To begin, let's discuss the tools required for effective pool skimming. A high-quality skimmer net attached to a telescopic pole is the primary tool you'll need. The net should be fine enough to capture even the most minor debris, while the pole should be long enough to reach all areas of your pool easily. Investing in a durable and reliable skimmer net will save you time and effort in the long run.

Now that you have the right equipment let's dive into the technique. Start by standing at one end of the pool, holding the telescopic pole with both hands. Extend the pole so the skimmer net reaches the water's surface and moves slowly and smoothly across the surface in a straight line. Be sure to overlap your strokes slightly to ensure no debris is missed.

As you skim, pay close attention to the corners and edges of the pool, as debris tends to accumulate in these areas. Use a gentle scooping motion to capture any stubborn debris clinging to the pool walls. Remember to empty your skimmer net frequently to maintain effectiveness and prevent debris from being reintroduced to the pool.

In addition to daily skimming, it's important to be proactive in addressing potential sources of debris. Trim overhanging trees and bushes, and consider using a pool cover when the pool is not in use. This will reduce the amount of debris entering your pool, help conserve water, and reduce evaporation.

To truly master the art of pool skimming, consistency is key. Make it a part of your daily routine, and you'll be rewarded with a sparkling clean pool that is always ready for a refreshing swim. By dedicating just a few minutes each day to this essential maintenance task, you'll be well on your way to achieving the inviting and pristine pool of your dreams.

Effective Brushing Techniques for a Clean Pool Surface

A sparkling clean pool looks inviting and ensures a healthy swimming environment for you and your loved ones. While skimming and vacuuming are essential components of pool maintenance, brushing the pool surface is pivotal in keeping it clean and algae-free. This section will explore effective brushing techniques that will help you maintain a pristine pool surface.

To begin with, it is crucial to choose the right brush for your pool. There are three main types of pool brushes: nylon, stainless steel, and a combination of both. Nylon brushes suit vinyl and fiberglass pools, while stainless steel brushes are ideal for concrete or plaster surfaces. For a versatile option, you can opt for a combination brush that works well on most pool surfaces.

Now that you have the appropriate brush, let's dive into the brushing techniques that will make a significant difference in your pool maintenance routine:

1. Start at the shallow end: Begin brushing your pool at the shallow end and gradually move towards the deep end. This systematic approach ensures you cover the entire pool surface without missing any spots.

2. Brush in a downward motion: When brushing the pool walls, always use a downward motion, starting from the waterline and moving towards the pool floor. This technique helps to dislodge dirt and debris, making it easier for the pool vacuum to remove them later.

3. Pay attention to corners and crevices: Algae and debris tend to accumulate in the corners and crevices of your pool. Make sure to thoroughly brush these areas to prevent algae growth and maintain a clean pool surface.

4. Brush the steps and ladders: Remember to brush the steps, ladders, and any other pool accessories that come in contact with the water. These areas are often overlooked but can harbor algae and bacteria if not cleaned regularly.

5. Maintain a consistent schedule: Consistency is key in pool maintenance. Ideally, you should brush your pool at least once weekly to keep the surface clean and free from algae buildup. However, you may need to brush more frequently during heavy use or after a storm.

6. Follow up with vacuuming: After brushing the pool surface, it is essential to vacuum the pool to remove the dislodged debris. This ensures that brushing efforts are not in vain and helps maintain a clean and healthy swimming environment.

By incorporating these effective brushing techniques into your pool maintenance routine, you will be well on your way to achieving a sparkling clean pool surface. The following section will discuss tips and tricks for vacuuming your pool to achieve optimal results.

Vacuuming Your Pool: Tips and Tricks for Optimal Results

Vacuuming your pool is essential to maintaining a clean and healthy swimming environment. Not only does it remove debris and dirt from the pool floor, but it also helps to prevent the growth of algae and bacteria. This section will explore tips and tricks to help you achieve optimal results when vacuuming your pool.

1. Choose the right vacuum for your pool: There are various types of pool vacuums available, including manual, automatic, and robotic models. Manual vacuums require more effort but offer greater control, while automatic and robotic vacuums are more convenient but may only reach some pool areas. When selecting a vacuum, consider your pool's size, shape, and specific cleaning needs.

2. Vacuum regularly: To maintain a clean pool, it's essential to vacuum at least once a week. This frequency may need to be increased during periods of heavy use or after storms introduce debris into the pool. Regular vacuuming helps to prevent the buildup of dirt and debris, making it easier to maintain a clean pool.

3. Follow a systematic pattern: When vacuuming your pool, it's important to follow a systematic pattern to ensure that all areas are covered. Start at the shallow end and work toward the deep end, overlapping each pass slightly to avoid missing any spots. Be sure to pay special attention to corners and areas around steps or ladders where debris accumulates.

4. Use slow, steady movements: Move a manual vacuum slowly and steadily across the pool floor. Rapid movements can stir up debris, making removing it harder and potentially clogging the vacuum. Moving slowly allows the vacuum to suction debris and dirt from the pool floor effectively.

5. Monitor the filter pressure: Monitor your pool's filter pressure gauge as you vacuum. If the pressure rises significantly, it may indicate that the vacuum is clogged or the filter needs cleaning. In either case, stop vacuuming and address the issue before continuing.

6. Remember to backwash: After vacuuming, it's important to backwash your pool's filter to remove any trapped debris and dirt. This will help to maintain the filter's efficiency and prolong its lifespan.

7. Consider using a leaf canister: If your pool accumulates many leaves and debris, consider using a leaf canister with your vacuum. This device captures leaves and debris before they reach the pool's filter, reducing the risk of clogs and making the vacuuming process more efficient.

By following these tips and tricks, you'll be well on your way to achieving a sparkling clean pool through effective vacuuming. Remember, a well-maintained pool looks great and provides a safe and enjoyable swimming experience for you and your family.

. . .

Balancing Skimming, Brushing, and Vacuuming in Your Pool Maintenance Routine

Maintaining a sparkling clean pool is not just about mastering unique techniques like skimming, brushing, and vacuuming. It is also about finding the perfect balance between these tasks in your pool maintenance routine. This section will discuss how to create a harmonious pool care schedule that incorporates all three techniques, ensuring your pool remains pristine all season long.

First and foremost, it is essential to understand that each technique serves a unique purpose in maintaining your pool's cleanliness. Skimming removes floating debris, brushing eliminates algae and dirt buildup on the pool's surfaces, and vacuuming clears away settled debris from the pool floor. By incorporating all three techniques into your routine, you can address various types of dirt and debris, leaving no stone unturned in your quest for a spotless pool.

To create a balanced pool maintenance routine, consider the following guidelines:

1. Skimming: Skimming should be performed daily or at least every other day. This frequent skimming will help prevent debris from sinking to the bottom of the pool, making vacuuming more manageable. Regular skimming can also improve water circulation and reduce the need for additional chemicals.

2. Brushing: Brushing should be done at least once a week, focusing on the pool's walls, steps, and other surfaces. Pay particular attention to areas with poor water circulation, as these spots are more prone to algae growth. Regular brushing will prevent algae and dirt buildup, keeping your pool's surfaces smooth and clean.

3. Vacuuming: Vacuuming should be performed at least once a week or more frequently if your pool receives heavy use or is surrounded by trees and plants that shed leaves and debris. Vacuuming removes settled debris from the pool floor, preventing it from becoming a breeding ground for algae and bacteria.

4. Timing: To maximize the effectiveness of your pool maintenance routine, try to stagger the tasks throughout the week. For example, skim on Monday, Wednesday, and Friday, brush on Tuesday, and vacuum on Thursday. This staggered schedule ensures that each technique is given adequate attention and helps maintain a consistently clean pool.

5. Adjust your routine: Remember that your pool's needs may change throughout the season. Factors such as weather, pool usage, and the surrounding environment can all impact the level of maintenance required. Be prepared to adjust your routine as needed, increasing or decreasing the frequency of skimming, brushing, and vacuuming to keep your pool in top shape.

By incorporating all three techniques into your pool maintenance routine and adjusting the frequency as needed, you can ensure that your pool remains a refreshing oasis for you and your family to enjoy all season long.

Achieving a Sparkling Clean Pool with Proper Techniques

In conclusion, a sparkling clean pool is not only visually appealing but also essential for the health and safety of swimmers. By mastering the art of skimming, brushing, and vacuuming, you can effectively maintain your pool and ensure it remains pristine. When combined and executed correctly, these techniques can make a world of difference in your pool's overall cleanliness and longevity.

Remember that consistency is key. Regularly skimming the pool surface will prevent debris from sinking and becoming more challenging to remove. Brushing your pool walls and floor at least once a week will help prevent the buildup of algae and other contaminants. Vacuuming your pool, either manually or with an automatic cleaner, will ensure that all debris is removed from the pool's surfaces and water.

Finding a balance in your pool maintenance routine that works best for you and your specific pool type. By incorporating these techniques into a regular schedule, you can save time, effort, and money in the long run. A well-maintained pool will require fewer chemicals and less frequent repairs, ultimately leading to a more enjoyable swimming experience for you and your family.

Chapter 4 Summary

1. Skimming, brushing, and vacuuming are essential for maintaining a clean and healthy swimming pool. Each technique serves a unique purpose and should be incorporated into a regular pool maintenance routine.

2. Skimming should be performed daily or at least every other day to remove floating debris from the pool surface, improve water circulation, and reduce the need for additional chemicals.

3. Brushing should be done at least once a week, focusing on the pool's walls, steps, and other surfaces. Regular brushing prevents algae and dirt buildup, keeping the pool surfaces smooth and clean.

4. Vacuuming should be performed at least once a week to remove settled debris from the pool floor, preventing it from becoming a breeding ground for algae and bacteria.

5. Choose the right tools for each technique, such as a high-quality skimmer net, the right brush for your pool surface, and a suitable vacuum for your pool's size and shape.

6. Follow a systematic pattern when performing each technique, ensuring that all pool areas are covered, and no spots are missed.

7. Adjust your pool maintenance routine as needed based on factors such as weather, pool usage, and the surrounding environment.

8. Consistency is key in maintaining a sparkling clean pool. By incorporating skimming, brushing, and vacuuming into a regular schedule, you can save time, effort, and money while ensuring a safe and enjoyable swimming experience for you and your family.

5. Maintaining Pool Filters and Pumps

Introduction to Pool Filters and Pumps Maintenance

In this chapter, we will dive into pool maintenance, focusing specifically on the essential components that keep your pool water clean and clear: filters and pumps. As a pool owner, you know the importance of maintaining a clean and healthy swimming environment. However, you should be fully aware of the crucial role that filters and pumps play in achieving this goal.

Pool filters and pumps work together to ensure your pool water remains free of debris, dirt, and contaminants. The pool pump circulates the water through the filter, which traps and removes any impurities before returning the clean water to the pool. This process is vital for maintaining a safe and enjoyable swimming experience for you and your family.

However, like any other mechanical system, pool filters and pumps require regular maintenance to function efficiently and effectively. Neglecting this aspect of pool care can lead to various issues, including poor water quality, reduced energy efficiency, and even costly damage to your pool equipment.

This chapter will provide a comprehensive guide to maintaining your pool filters and pumps. We will begin by exploring the different types of pool filters and pumps available on the market, helping you understand each system's unique maintenance requirements. Next, we will discuss routine cleaning and maintenance tasks to keep your filters and pumps in top condition. We will also address common pool pump issues and provide troubleshooting tips to help you quickly identify and resolve any problems that may arise.

Finally, we will offer valuable tips for extending the lifespan of your pool filters and pumps, ensuring that your pool system remains clean and efficient for years to come. By the end of this chapter, you will be equipped with the knowledge and skills necessary to maintain your pool filters and pumps like a pro, providing a pristine swimming environment for your friends and family to enjoy.

So, let's dive in and discover the secrets to maintaining a clean and efficient pool system through properly caring for your filters and pumps!

Understanding the Different Types of Pool Filters and Pumps

Before diving into the specifics of maintaining your pool filters and pumps, you must have a solid understanding of the equipment available. This knowledge will not only help you choose the best system for your pool but also ensure that you're well-equipped to handle any maintenance tasks that come your way. In this section, we'll explore the three main types of pool filters and the two primary types of pool pumps, highlighting their unique features and benefits.

Pool Filters

The water circulation and filtration system in a pool works in the following way:

1. Water enters the pool through the main drain and the skimmer.

2. The water is then pulled into the pool pump, which creates a suction that draws the water through the pool filter.

3. The pool filter removes dirt, debris, and other contaminants from the water, before it is returned to the pool.

4. The filtered water is then returned to the pool through the return jets.

5. The process of circulating and filtering the water helps to keep it clean and clear, and prevents the growth of algae and other harmful bacteria.

There are three main types of pool filters:

1. Sand Filters: Sand filters are popular among pool owners due to their affordability and ease of use. They use a bed of specially graded sand to trap dirt and debris as water flows through the filter. Over time, the sand becomes clogged with contaminants, requiring backwashing to clean it. Sand filters are generally low-maintenance and can last several years before needing a sand replacement.

2. Cartridge Filters: Cartridge filters utilize a cylindrical cartridge made of pleated polyester or other synthetic

materials to capture debris. These filters are known for their energy efficiency and ability to filter out smaller particles than sand filters. Cartridge filters require less frequent cleaning, as they can be easily removed and hosed down when necessary. However, they typically have a higher upfront cost and may need more frequent cartridge replacements.

3. Diatomaceous Earth (DE) Filters: DE filters are considered the most effective at trapping the tiniest particles, providing the most transparent water. They use fine powder from fossilized diatoms to coat grids or filter elements. The DE powder captures debris and contaminants as water passes through the filter. DE filters require regular backwashing and periodic DE powder replacement, making them slightly more labor-intensive than other filter types.

Pool Pumps

1. Single-Speed Pumps: Single-speed pumps are the most basic type of pool pump, operating at a constant speed whenever turned on. While they're usually the most affordable option, they can be less energy-efficient than other pump types, as they only allow for adjustments based on your pool's needs.

2. Variable-Speed Pumps: Variable-speed pumps offer greater energy efficiency and flexibility, allowing you to adjust the pump's speed according to your pool's requirements. These pumps use a permanent magnet motor, which enables them to operate at different speeds while consuming less energy. Although they have a higher upfront cost, variable-speed pumps can save you money in the long run due to their reduced energy consumption.

Now that you better understand the different types of pool filters and pumps, you're ready to tackle the maintenance tasks that will keep your pool system running smoothly. In the next section, we'll discuss routine cleaning and maintenance for your pool filters, ensuring your pool stays clean and inviting all season long.

Routine Cleaning and Maintenance of Pool Filters

A sparkling, crystal-clear pool is every pool owner's dream, and the key to achieving this lies in regularly cleaning and maintaining pool filters. Pool filters play a crucial role in maintaining the cleanliness and clarity of your pool water by trapping dirt, debris, and other impurities. This section will discuss the essential steps for routine cleaning and maintenance of pool filters, ensuring that your pool remains a refreshing oasis for you and your family.

To begin with, it's essential to understand that there are three main types of pool filters: sand, cartridge, and diatomaceous earth (DE) filters. While each type has unique cleaning and maintenance requirements, some general guidelines apply.

1. Regular Inspection: Regardless of the type of filter you have, it's essential to inspect it regularly for any signs of wear, damage, or clogging. This will help you identify potential issues before they escalate and affect your pool's water quality. Make it a habit to check your filter at least once a month or more frequently during periods of heavy pool usage.

2. Backwashing: Sand and DE filters require periodic backwashing to remove accumulated dirt and debris. This process involves reversing the water flow through the filter and flushing out the trapped contaminants. Backwashing should be performed when the pressure gauge on your filter indicates a seven to ten psi increase over the normal operating pressure or at least once a month. Be sure to

follow the manufacturer's instructions for your specific filter model.

3. Cartridge Cleaning: Regular cleaning is necessary for cartridge filters to maintain optimal performance. Remove the cartridge from the filter housing and use a garden hose to spray off any dirt and debris. For more thorough cleaning, you can also soak the cartridge in a filter cleaner solution, following the manufacturer's recommendations. Cartridge filters should be cleaned every two to four weeks, depending on pool usage and debris present.

4. DE Filter Maintenance: Besides backwashing, DE filters require the periodic addition of fresh diatomaceous earth. After backwashing, add the recommended amount of DE powder to your skimmer, which will then be distributed to the filter grids. This process helps maintain the filter's efficiency and effectively removes impurities from your pool water.

5. Filter Replacement: Over time, all types of pool filters will experience wear and tear, eventually requiring replacement. Sand filters typically need new sand every five to seven years, while cartridge filters should be replaced every one to two years, depending on usage and maintenance. DE filter grids should be inspected annually for damage and replaced as needed.

By adhering to these routine cleaning and maintenance guidelines, you can ensure that your pool filters continue functioning at their best, providing clean, clear, and inviting pool water. Remember, a well-maintained pool filter is the foundation of a healthy and enjoyable swimming environment.

Troubleshooting Common Pool Pump Issues

Pool pumps are the heart of your swimming pool's circulation system, working tirelessly to keep the water clean and clear. However, like any mechanical device, they can encounter issues from time to time. This section will explore some common pool pump problems and offer practical solutions to help you troubleshoot and resolve these issues easily.

1. Noisy Pump Operation

A noisy pool pump can be quite an annoyance, often a sign that something is amiss. The most common causes of a noisy pump include:

- Clogged or obstructed impeller: A debris buildup in the impeller can cause the pump to work harder and produce more noise. To fix this issue, turn off the pump, disconnect it from the power source, and carefully remove and clean the impeller.

- Worn or damaged bearings: Over time, the bearings in your pool pump can wear out or become damaged, causing excessive noise. In this case, you must replace the bearings to restore quiet operation.

2. Pump Not Priming

If your pool pump is not priming, it cannot draw water from the pool and push it through the filter system. Common causes of this issue include:

- Blocked or clogged skimmer baskets and pump strainer: Ensure that both the skimmer and pump strainer are clean and debris-free.

- Air leaks in the suction line: Inspect the suction line for any cracks or loose connections that could allow air to enter the system. Repair or replace any damaged components as needed.

- Low water level: If the water level in your pool is too low, the pump may struggle to prime. Ensure that the water level is at the appropriate height, typically halfway up the skimmer opening.

3. Pump Losing Prime

If your pool pump loses prime while running, it can reduce water flow and diminish filtration efficiency. Common causes of a pump losing its prime include:

- Air leaks in the suction line: As mentioned earlier, air leaks can cause the pump to lose its prime. Inspect and repair any leaks in the suction line.

- Damaged or worn impeller: A damaged impeller can reduce the pump's ability to maintain prime. Inspect the impeller for wear or damage and replace it if necessary.

4. Reduced Water Flow

A decrease in water flow can be caused by several factors, including:

- Clogged or dirty filter: A dirty filter can impede water flow. Clean or replace the filter as needed to restore proper water flow.

- Obstructed return lines: Check the return lines for any blockages or obstructions and remove any debris as necessary.

- Pump motor issues: If the pump motor is not running at full speed or malfunctioning, it can reduce water flow. Consult a pool professional to diagnose and repair any motor issues.

Addressing these common pool pump issues ensures that your pool's circulation system remains efficient and effective. Regular maintenance and prompt attention to any problems will help extend the lifespan of your pool pump and keep your pool water clean and inviting.

Tips for Extending the Lifespan of Your Pool Filters and Pumps

Pool filters and pumps are the heart and lungs of your swimming pool, working tirelessly to keep the water clean, clear, and inviting. To ensure that these essential components continue to function optimally, it's crucial to take steps to extend their lifespan. In this section, we'll share some practical tips to help you get the most out of your pool filters and pumps.

1. Regularly inspect and clean your filters: As a pool owner, staying on top of filter maintenance is essential. Regularly inspect your filters for signs of wear, tear, or damage, and clean them as needed. This will help maintain the efficiency of your pool's filtration system and prolong the life of your filters.

2. Don't run your pump 24/7: While it may be tempting to keep your pool pump running constantly, doing so can lead to unnecessary wear and tear on the motor. Instead, establish a schedule for running your pump, typically between eight to twelve hours daily, depending on your pool's size and usage. This will help to conserve energy and extend the life of your pump.

3. Keep an eye on water chemistry: Maintaining balanced water chemistry is crucial for the health of your pool and its equipment. Imbalanced water can cause corrosion, scaling, and other issues that damage your filters and pumps. Regularly test your pool water and adjust as needed to keep it within the recommended ranges for pH, alkalinity, and sanitizer levels.

4. Lubricate moving parts: Like any mechanical equipment, your pool pump requires regular lubrication to keep its moving parts functioning smoothly. Consult your pump's owner's manual for guidance on the proper lubrication schedule and the type of lubricant. This simple maintenance task can go a long way in extending the life of your pump.

5. Replace worn or damaged parts promptly: If you notice any signs of wear or damage on your pool filters or pump components, it's essential to address these issues promptly. Delaying repairs can lead to more significant problems and prevent your equipment from failing prematurely.

6. Protect your equipment from the elements: Exposure to harsh weather conditions can affect your pool filters and pumps. Install a protective cover or enclosure around your equipment to protect it from the elements. This will help to prevent rust, corrosion, and other weather-related damage.

7. Schedule professional maintenance: While there's a lot you can do on your own to maintain your pool filters and pumps, it's also essential to schedule regular professional maintenance. A skilled technician can spot potential issues before they become major problems and ensure your equipment runs efficiently.

By following these tips, you can help to extend the lifespan of your pool filters and pumps, ensuring that your pool remains clean, clear, and enjoyable for years to come. Remember, preventative maintenance goes a long way in keeping your pool's essential components in top shape.

Ensuring a Clean and Efficient Pool System

In conclusion, maintaining a clean and efficient pool system is essential for your swimming pool's overall health and enjoyment. Proper care and attention to your pool filters and pumps will not only guarantee crystal-clear water but also extend the lifespan of your equipment, saving you time and money in the long run.

Throughout this chapter, we have explored the different types of pool filters and pumps, discussed the importance of routine cleaning and maintenance, and provided troubleshooting tips for common pool pump issues. By following these guidelines and incorporating them into your regular pool care routine, you can ensure that your pool remains a refreshing and inviting oasis for you, your family, and your guests.

Finally, it's important to remember that pool maintenance is ongoing. By staying vigilant and dedicating time to regularly inspect, clean, and maintain your pool filters and pumps, you'll be rewarded with a beautiful, safe, and enjoyable swimming environment for years to come. So, roll up your sleeves, grab your tools, and dive into pool maintenance with confidence and enthusiasm. Your sparkling pool will thank you for it!

Chapter 5 Summary

1. Pool filters and pumps are essential components of a pool system, working together to keep the water clean and clear.

2. There are three main types of pool filters (sand, cartridge, and DE filters) and two primary types of pool pumps (single-speed and variable-speed), each with unique features and maintenance requirements.

3. Regular inspection and cleaning of pool filters are crucial for maintaining water quality and extending the lifespan of the equipment.

4. Sand and DE filters require periodic backwashing, while cartridge filters require regular cleaning and occasional replacement.

5. Common pool pump issues include noisy operation, pump not priming, pump losing prime.

6. Introduction to Balancing Pool Water Chemistry

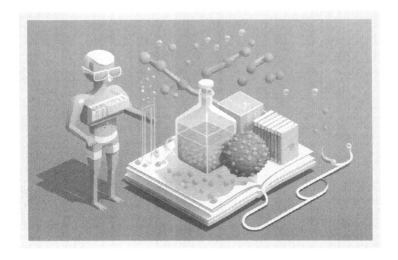

This chapter will dive into the fascinating world of pool water chemistry and explore its importance in maintaining a healthy and enjoyable swimming environment. Whether you are a new pool owner or a seasoned veteran, understanding the basics of pool water chemistry is essential for keeping your pool crystal clear and safe for all swimmers.

Balancing pool water chemistry is a delicate dance that requires attention to detail and a solid understanding of the key components involved. When properly balanced, your pool water will look inviting and provide a comfortable and safe environment for swimmers. On the other hand, imbalanced pool water can lead to many issues, ranging from unpleasant odors and skin irritation to damaged pool equipment and surfaces.

This chapter will cover the essential aspects of pool water chemistry, including the key components that need to be monitored and adjusted. We will also discuss the importance of regular testing and guide how to adjust chemicals for optimal balance. Additionally, we will address common issues that can arise in pool water chemistry and offer solutions to help you maintain a healthy and balanced pool environment.

So, grab your test kit and put on your lab goggles as we embark on this exciting journey to mastering the art of balancing pool water chemistry. By the end of this chapter, you will be well-equipped with the knowledge and confidence needed to ensure your pool remains a sparkling oasis for all to enjoy.

Understanding the Key Components of Pool Water Chemistry

To maintain a sparkling, healthy pool, it's essential to understand the key components of pool water chemistry. By grasping the fundamentals, you'll be better equipped to address any imbalances and ensure a safe swimming environment for you and your guests. In this section, we'll explore the four primary elements of pool water chemistry: pH, total alkalinity, calcium hardness, and sanitizer levels.

a) pH: The pH scale measures the acidity or alkalinity of your pool water, ranging from zero (highly acidic) to fourteen (highly alkaline), with seven being neutral. The ideal pH level for pool water is between 7.4 and 7.6, which is slightly alkaline and matches the natural pH of our eyes. Maintaining the correct pH level is crucial for the effectiveness of sanitizers and for preventing corrosion or scaling on pool surfaces and equipment.

b) Total Alkalinity (TA): Total alkalinity refers to measuring your pool water's ability to neutralize acids, acting as a buffer to prevent rapid pH fluctuations. A proper TA level helps maintain stable pH levels and prevents issues like etching, staining, and cloudy water. The ideal TA range for most pools is between 80 and 120 parts per million (ppm).

c) Calcium Hardness: Calcium hardness measures the amount of dissolved calcium in your pool water. This component is essential for preventing damage to your pool surfaces and equipment. Low calcium hardness levels can lead to the etching and pitting of surfaces, while high levels can cause scaling and cloudy water. The recommended calcium hardness range is between 200 and 400 ppm for plaster pools and 175 to 225 ppm for vinyl, fiberglass, and painted pools.

d) Sanitizer Levels: Sanitizers, such as chlorine or bromine, are vital for killing bacteria, viruses, and algae in your pool water. Maintaining proper sanitizer levels ensures a safe and healthy swimming environment. The ideal chlorine level is between one and three ppm, while the recommended bromine level is between three and five ppm.

Now that you have a solid understanding of the key components of pool water chemistry, you're well on your way to mastering the art of pool maintenance. In the next section, we'll discuss how to test and monitor your pool's chemical levels to ensure they remain within the ideal ranges for a clean, balanced, and inviting pool.

Testing and Monitoring Your Pool's Chemical Levels

To ensure a safe and enjoyable swimming experience, testing and monitoring your pool's chemical levels is essential. This helps maintain the perfect balance of pool water chemistry and prevents common issues such as algae growth, cloudy water, and damage to pool equipment. This section will discuss the importance of testing and monitoring, the various methods available, and how often you should perform these tasks.

Why Test and Monitor Your Pool's Chemical Levels?

Regular testing and monitoring of your pool's chemical levels are crucial for several reasons:

1. Safety: Balanced pool water chemistry ensures a safe swimming environment, preventing skin and eye irritation and reducing the risk of waterborne illnesses.

2. Aesthetics: A well-maintained pool with balanced chemical levels will have clear, sparkling water inviting to swimmers.

3. Equipment longevity: Properly balanced pool water helps prevent corrosion and scaling on pool equipment, such as pumps, filters, and heaters, thus extending their lifespan.

4. Cost-effectiveness: Regular testing and monitoring can save you money in the long run by preventing costly pool equipment repairs and replacements.

Methods for Testing Pool Water

Several methods are available for testing your pool's chemical levels, each with advantages and disadvantages. The most common methods include the following:

1. Test strips are easy-to-use, disposable strips that change color when dipped into the pool water. By comparing the strip's color to the provided color chart, you can determine the levels of various chemicals in your pool. Test strips are affordable and widely available, but they may not be as accurate as other methods.

2. Liquid test kits: These kits use reagents, which are chemical solutions that react with the pool water to produce a color change. You can determine the chemical levels in

your pool by adding a few drops of the reagent to a water sample and comparing the resulting color to a color chart. Liquid test kits are generally more accurate than test strips but may require more time and effort.

3. Digital testers: These electronic devices provide quick and accurate readings of your pool's chemical levels. While they are more expensive than other testing methods, digital testers are easy to use and offer precise results.

How Often Should You Test and Monitor Your Pool's Chemical Levels?

Generally, you should test and monitor your pool's chemical levels at least once a week. However, it is advisable to test more frequently during periods of heavy use or after significant weather events, such as rainstorms. Additionally, it is essential to test your pool water after adding chemicals to ensure the levels are within the recommended range.

In conclusion, regular testing and monitoring of your pool's chemical levels are vital for maintaining a safe, enjoyable, and cost-effective swimming environment. By familiarizing yourself with the various testing methods and adhering to a consistent testing schedule, you can ensure that your pool remains a healthy and balanced oasis for all to enjoy.

Adjusting Chemicals for Optimal Balance

A well-balanced pool is not only a delight to swim in, but it also ensures the longevity of your pool equipment and the health of your swimmers. This section will discuss the steps you need to take to adjust the chemicals in your pool for optimal balance. By following these guidelines, you can create a safe and enjoyable aquatic environment for everyone.

Before we dive into the specifics of adjusting chemicals, it's important to remember that safety should always be your top priority. Always read and follow the manufacturer's instructions for any pool chemicals you use, and wear appropriate protective gear, such as gloves and goggles, when handling them.

Now, let's explore the process of adjusting your pool's chemical levels:

1. Test your pool water: The first step in adjusting your pool's chemical balance is to test the water using a reliable pool test kit. This will provide accurate readings of your pool's pH, total alkalinity, calcium hardness, and sanitizer levels. It's essential to test your pool water regularly, ideally at least once a week, to ensure that the chemical levels remain within the recommended ranges.

2. Adjust the pH level: The pH level of your pool water measures its acidity or alkalinity. A balanced pH level should be between 7.4 and 7.6. If your pool's pH is too low (acidic), you can raise it by adding a pH increaser, such as sodium carbonate. If the pH is too high (alkaline), you can lower it by adding a pH decreaser, such as sodium bisulfate. Always follow the manufacturer's instructions for the correct dosage and application method.

3. Balance the total alkalinity: Total alkalinity measures the water's ability to buffer pH changes. Maintaining proper alkalinity levels helps to stabilize the pH, preventing rapid fluctuations. The ideal alkalinity range is between 80 and 120 parts per million (ppm). Add an alkalinity increaser, such as sodium bicarbonate, to increase total alkalinity. To decrease total alkalinity, use a product specifically designed to lower alkalinities, such as muriatic acid or sodium bisulfate.

4. Manage calcium hardness: Calcium hardness refers to the amount of calcium in your pool water. Proper calcium hardness levels prevent scaling and protect your pool surfaces and equipment. The recommended calcium hardness range is between 200 and 400 ppm. Add calcium hardness increaser, such as calcium chloride, to increase calcium hardness. You can either partially drain and refill your pool with softer water or use a commercial hardness reducer to decrease calcium hardness.

5. Maintain sanitizer levels: Sanitizers, such as chlorine or bromine, are essential for keeping your pool water clean and free of harmful bacteria and algae. Regularly test your sanitizer levels and adjust them to maintain the recommended range. The ideal range for chlorine pools is one-three ppm, while bromine pools should maintain a level of three-five ppm. To increase sanitizer levels, add the appropriate sanitizer product, and to decrease levels, you can either wait for the sanitizer to dissipate naturally or use a chemical reducer.

By carefully monitoring and adjusting your pool's chemical levels, you can maintain a well-balanced aquatic environment that is safe and enjoyable for all. Consistency is key; regular testing and adjustments will help you prevent common issues and keep your pool in tip-top shape.

Example with numbers

Here is an example of chemical dosing for a typical 10,000-gallon pool:

Chlorine

The recommended level for free chlorine in a pool is between one and three parts per million (ppm). To raise the chlorine level by one ppm in a 10,000-gallon pool, you would need to add approximately 0.65 fluid ounces (nineteen mL) of liquid chlorine, or 1.3 ounces (thirty-seven grams) of granular chlorine.

pH Adjuster

The recommended pH range for a pool is between 7.2 and 7.8. To raise the pH level by 0.2 in a 10,000-gallon pool, you would need to add approximately five ounces (142 grams) of sodium carbonate (pH increaser). To lower the pH level by 0.2, you would need to add approximately 1.25 ounces (thirty six grams) of sodium bisulfate (pH decreaser).

Alkalinity Adjuster

The recommended range for total alkalinity in a pool is between 80 and 120 ppm. To raise the alkalinity level by ten ppm in a 10,000-gallon pool, you would need to add approximately 1.25 pounds (567 grams) of sodium bicarbonate (alkalinity increaser).

5. Common Issues and Solutions in Pool Water Chemistry

Even the most diligent pool owners may need help with their pool water chemistry from time to time. This section will discuss some of the most common problems that can arise and provide practical solutions to help you maintain a healthy and balanced pool environment. By proactively addressing these issues as they occur, you can prevent more significant problems from developing and ensure that your pool remains a safe and enjoyable space for everyone.

Cloudy or Discolored Water

One of the most common issues pool owners face is cloudy or discolored water. This can be caused by a variety of factors, including improper chemical balance, poor filtration, or the presence of algae or other contaminants. To address this issue, first, test your pool's chemical levels and adjust them as needed. If the problem persists, consider cleaning or replacing your pool's filter, as a clogged or worn-out filter may not effectively remove debris and contaminants from the water. Finally, if you suspect algae may be the culprit, treat your pool with an appropriate algaecide to eliminate the problem.

Chlorine Odor or Eye Irritation

A strong chlorine smell or eye irritation can indicate that your pool's chemical balance is off. Contrary to popular belief, a strong chlorine odor does not necessarily mean too much chlorine in the water. Instead, it often indicates the presence of chloramines, formed when chlorine reacts with organic matter such as sweat, oils, and urine. To resolve this issue, you may need to "shock" your pool by adding a large dose of chlorine or a non-chlorine shock treatment to break down the chloramines and restore the proper chemical balance.

Green water

Green pool water is typically a sign of algae growth, which can occur when your pool's chemical balance is off or the circulation and filtration systems are not functioning correctly. First, test and adjust your pool's chemical levels as needed to treat a green pool. Then, brush the pool surfaces to remove algae clinging to the walls and floor. Follow this by adding an algaecide and running your pool's filter continuously for twenty-four to forty-eight hours to remove the dead algae from the water. Be sure to clean or backwash your filter as needed during this process.

Scaling or Staining

Scaling or staining on your pool's surfaces can be caused by an imbalance in your pool's calcium hardness or pH levels. High calcium hardness can lead to calcium deposits, while low pH levels can cause metal stains. To address scaling, test your pool's calcium hardness and pH levels and adjust them as needed. If scaling persists, consider using a scale inhibitor to prevent further buildup. For metal stains, you can use a metal sequestrant to help remove the stains and prevent future occurrences.

By being aware of these common pool water chemistry issues and taking the appropriate steps to address them, you can maintain a healthy and balanced pool environment for all to enjoy. Regularly testing and monitoring your pool's chemical levels are crucial to preventing these problems and ensuring that your pool remains a safe and inviting oasis.

Maintaining a Healthy and Balanced Pool Environment

In conclusion, maintaining a healthy and balanced pool environment is essential for ensuring the safety and enjoyment of all who use it. By understanding the key components of pool water chemistry, regularly testing and monitoring chemical levels, and making necessary adjustments, you can create an inviting and sanitary aquatic oasis for friends and family to enjoy.

A well-maintained pool not only looks and feels great but also extends the life of your pool equipment and reduces the risk of costly repairs. By staying proactive and addressing any chemical imbalances or issues as they arise, you can keep your pool in peak condition and prevent problems from escalating.

Remember that consistency is key when it comes to pool maintenance. Establishing a routine for testing and adjusting chemical levels will help you stay on top of your pool's needs and ensure that it remains a safe and enjoyable space for everyone.

Ultimately, the time and effort you invest in maintaining your pool's water chemistry will pay off in the form of a beautiful, crystal-clear swimming pool that provides endless hours of relaxation and enjoyment.

Chapter 6 Summary

1. Balancing pool water chemistry is essential for maintaining a healthy and enjoyable swimming environment, preventing unpleasant odors, skin irritation, and damage to pool equipment and surfaces.

2. The four primary elements of pool water chemistry are pH, total alkalinity, calcium hardness, and sanitizer levels. Understanding these components is crucial for proper pool maintenance.

3. Regularly testing and monitoring your pool's chemical levels is vital for ensuring a safe swimming environment, preventing common issues, and extending the lifespan of pool equipment.

4. Various methods for testing pool water include test strips, liquid test kits, and digital testers. Each method has advantages and disadvantages, so choose the one that best suits your needs and preferences.

5. Adjusting chemicals for optimal balance involves testing your pool water, adjusting pH levels, balancing total alkalinity, managing calcium hardness, and maintaining sanitizer levels. Safety should always be a priority when handling pool chemicals.

6. Common issues in pool water chemistry include cloudy or discolored water, chlorine odor or eye irritation, green water, and scaling or staining. Being proactive and addressing these issues as they occur can prevent more significant problems from developing.

7. Consistency is key when it comes to pool maintenance. Establishing a routine for testing and adjusting chemical levels will help you stay on top of your pool's needs and

ensure that it remains a safe and enjoyable space for everyone.

7. Algae Prevention and Treatment

Picture this: You've been anticipating a relaxing day by the pool, soaking up the sun and enjoying the refreshing water. As you approach your backyard oasis, you're greeted by a murky, green pool that looks more like a swamp than a place to swim. The culprit? Algae.

Algae are microscopic, plant-like organisms that thrive in damp environments and can be a pool owner's worst nightmare. These tiny invaders can transform your pristine pool into a slimy, uninviting mess in days. But fear not! With the proper knowledge and tools, you can prevent and treat algae infestations, ensuring your pool remains crystal clear and ready for a swim.

Before we dive into the various methods of algae prevention and treatment, it's essential to understand what algae are and why they pose a problem for pool maintenance. Algae are photosynthetic organisms that can grow and multiply rapidly under the right conditions. They can enter your pool through various means, such as wind, rain, or even on the swimsuits of your guests. Once they've entered your pool, they can quickly multiply, causing unsightly and potentially harmful blooms.

There are several reasons why algae are undesirable in your pool. Firstly, they can create a slippery and dangerous surface on pool walls and floors, increasing the risk of accidents. Secondly, they can clog your pool's filter system, reducing efficiency and causing costly repairs. Lastly, and perhaps most importantly, algae can negatively impact the water quality, making it unsafe for swimming and causing skin and eye irritation.

Now that we've established why algae are the enemy, it's time to learn how to identify the different types of algae that can invade your pool and the essential pool maintenance practices for keeping them at bay. Stay tuned as we dive deeper into the world of algae prevention and treatment, ensuring that your pool remains a sparkling, algae-free haven for you and your loved ones.

Identifying Different Types of Algae in Your Pool

Before diving into the battle against algae, knowing your opponent is essential. Algae come in various forms, requiring a slightly different approach to treatment and prevention. This section will discuss the most common types of algae found in swimming pools and how to identify them.

Green Algae

Green algae, scientifically known as Chlorophyta, is the most common algae found in pools. It can appear as a greenish tint to your pool water or as green patches on the walls and floor. Green algae thrive in poor water circulation, inadequate sanitation, and imbalanced water chemistry. If left untreated, green algae can quickly multiply, turning your pool into a murky, uninviting swamp.

Yellow or Mustard Algae

Yellow algae, also known as mustard algae (Phaeophyta), is a more stubborn and persistent type of algae. It appears as yellow or brownish patches on the pool walls, floor, or other surfaces. Mustard algae can be challenging to eliminate, as it is resistant to regular chlorine treatments and tends to cling to pool surfaces, even after brushing. This type of algae is more common in shaded pool areas and requires a more aggressive approach to treatment and prevention.

Black Algae

Black algae (Cyanobacteria) is the least common but most challenging type of algae to eradicate from your pool. It appears as dark black or blue-green spots on the pool surfaces, often with a slimy or slippery texture. Black algae have deep, strong roots that penetrate the pool's surfaces, making them highly resistant to regular treatments. They are most commonly found in plaster or concrete pools, as their rough surfaces provide an ideal environment for the algae to anchor themselves.

Pink Algae

Pink algae, also known as pink slime (Mycobacterium), is not an algae but a type of bacteria that can grow in your pool. It appears as a pink, slimy substance on pool surfaces, equipment, and your pool's plumbing system. While pink algae are not harmful to swimmers, they can clog your pool's filtration system and create an unsightly appearance.

Now that you are familiar with the different types of algae that can invade your pool, you are better equipped to tackle the problem head-on. The following sections will discuss essential pool maintenance practices for algae prevention and various chemical and non-chemical methods to combat algae growth. With the proper knowledge and tools, you can maintain a crystal clear and algae-free pool for you and your family to enjoy.

Essential Pool Maintenance Practices for Algae Prevention

Algae, the unwelcome guest in your pool, can turn a refreshing oasis into a murky, uninviting mess. But fear not, pool owners! You can prevent algae from gaining a foothold in your swimming haven with a few essential pool maintenance practices. This section will explore the key steps to keep your pool crystal clear and algae-free.

First and foremost, maintaining proper water circulation is crucial in preventing algae growth. Stagnant water is a breeding ground for these pesky organisms, so keeping your pool water moving is essential. Ensure that your pool pump and filter are functioning correctly, and run them for at least eight to twelve hours a day. Regularly check and clean the skimmer baskets, pump baskets, and pool filters to prevent debris buildup, which can hinder water flow. Additionally, using a pool brush to manually clean the pool walls, floor, and steps at least once a week will help dislodge any algae spores before they have a chance to multiply.

Next, it's vital to keep your pool's water chemistry balanced. Algae thrive in poorly balanced water, so regular testing and adjusting your pool's pH, alkalinity, and sanitizer levels are necessary. Aim to maintain a pH level between 7.2 and 7.6, alkalinity between 80 and 120 parts per million (ppm), and a sanitizer level (chlorine or bromine) within the recommended range for your specific pool type. Regularly shocking your pool with a strong sanitizer dose will also help kill off any lingering algae spores.

Another essential practice for algae prevention is maintaining a clean and debris-free pool environment. Organic debris, such as leaves, grass, and dirt, can introduce algae spores into your pool and give them the nutrients they need to grow. Make a habit of skimming your pool surface daily to remove floating debris, and use a pool vacuum to clean the pool floor at least once a week. Keeping the area around your pool clean and vegetation-free will also help minimize the introduction of algae spores.

Lastly, consider using an algaecide as part of your regular pool maintenance routine. Algaecides are chemicals specifically designed to inhibit algae growth and can be an effective preventative measure when used correctly. Be sure to follow the manufacturer's instructions for the proper dosage and application method, as overuse can lead to foaming or other undesirable side effects.

Chemical Solutions for Algae Control and Elimination

Now that we've covered the basics of algae and preventive measures, it's time to dive into the world of chemical solutions for algae control and elimination. While it's always best to prevent algae growth in the first place, sometimes it's necessary to take more aggressive action to reclaim your pool from these pesky invaders. This section will explore the most effective chemical treatments for combating algae and restoring your pool to its pristine, crystal-clear state.

Chlorine: The First Line of Defense

Chlorine is the most common and widely used pool sanitizer because it's highly effective at killing algae and other microorganisms. When properly maintained, a chlorine level of one-three parts per million (ppm) is usually sufficient to keep algae at bay. However, if you're dealing with an active algae outbreak, you'll need to "shock" your pool with a higher dose of chlorine to eradicate the problem. Aim for a level of ten to twenty ppm, and follow the manufacturer's instructions for your specific pool shock product.

Algaecides: A Potent Ally in the Fight Against Algae

Algaecides are specially formulated chemicals designed to target and eliminate algae. They work in tandem with chlorine, enhancing its effectiveness and providing an extra layer of protection against algae growth. Several types of algaecides are available, including copper-based and quaternary ammonium compounds. Each has its unique benefits and drawbacks, so choosing the right one for your specific algae problem is essential. Follow the manufacturer's recommendations to ensure the best results.

Phosphate Removers: Starving Algae of Their Food Source

Phosphates are a primary food source for algae, and high phosphate levels in your pool can contribute to persistent algae problems. Using a phosphate remover can effectively starve algae and inhibit their growth. These products work by binding to phosphates and making them insoluble, allowing your pool filter to remove them from the water. Regularly testing your pool's phosphate levels and using a phosphate remover as needed can help keep algae in check and maintain optimal water quality.

Balancing Pool Chemistry: The Key to Effective Algae Control

While chlorine, algaecides, and phosphate removers are all powerful tools in the fight against algae, they will only be effective if your pool's overall chemistry is balanced. It's crucial to regularly test and adjust your pool's pH, alkalinity, and calcium hardness levels to ensure that your chemical treatments can work their magic. Aim for a pH level between 7.2 and 7.6, total alkalinity between 80 and 120 ppm, and calcium hardness between 200 and 400 ppm for the best results.

Non-Chemical Methods to Combat Algae Growth

While chemical solutions are often the go-to method for controlling and eliminating algae, it's essential to remember that there are also effective non-chemical approaches to keep your pool algae-free. Incorporating these natural strategies into your pool maintenance routine can reduce your reliance on chemicals and create a more eco-friendly swimming environment. Let's dive into some of the best non-chemical methods to combat algae growth in your pool.

Proper Circulation and Filtration

One of the most critical factors in preventing algae growth is ensuring that your pool has adequate circulation and filtration. Stagnant water is a breeding ground for algae, so keeping the water moving is essential. Ensure your pool pump and filter are running efficiently and for the recommended amount of time each day, typically eight to twelve hours. Regularly clean and backwash your filter to maintain optimal performance. Additionally, aim to direct your pool's return jets in a way that promotes even water circulation throughout the entire pool.

Regular Pool Cleaning

A clean pool is less susceptible to algae growth. Make it a habit to skim your pool's surface daily to remove debris, such as leaves and twigs, which can contribute to algae growth. Vacuum your pool at least once weekly to remove dirt and organic matter from the pool floor and walls. Remember to brush the pool walls, steps, and ladders, as these are common areas where algae can cling and grow. Keeping your pool clean will create an environment that's less inviting to algae.

Balanced Pool Water

While not entirely chemical-free, maintaining balanced pool water prevents algae growth. Regularly test your pool water to ensure the pH, alkalinity, and calcium hardness levels are within the recommended ranges. Balanced water chemistry helps prevent algae and ensures the effectiveness of any chemical treatments you may use.

Use of Solar Pool Covers

Solar pool covers can be an effective non-chemical method to combat algae growth. Covering your pool when it's not in use will reduce the amount of sunlight that penetrates the water. Since algae require sunlight to grow, limiting their access to sunlight can help prevent their growth. Additionally, solar pool covers help to retain heat and reduce water evaporation, providing added benefits to your pool maintenance routine.

Incorporating these non-chemical methods into your pool maintenance routine can effectively combat algae growth and maintain a crystal-clear, inviting swimming environment. Remember that prevention is always better than cure, so stay consistent with your pool care practices to keep algae at bay.

Maintaining a Crystal Clear and Algae-Free Pool

In conclusion, maintaining a crystal clear and algae-free pool is essential for the aesthetic appeal of your backyard oasis and the health and safety of those who enjoy it. Throughout this chapter, we have delved into the world of algae, understanding its nature, identifying its various types, and exploring chemical and non-chemical methods to prevent and treat its growth in your pool.

By implementing essential pool maintenance practices, such as regular cleaning, proper water circulation, and balanced water chemistry, you can effectively prevent algae growth in your pool. It is crucial to stay vigilant and consistent with these practices, as algae can quickly take over your pool if given the opportunity.

When faced with an algae infestation, we have discussed various chemical solutions, such as algaecides and chlorine shock treatments, which can effectively control and eliminate algae growth. However, using these chemicals responsibly and according to the manufacturer's instructions is essential to ensure the safety of swimmers and the environment.

Ultimately, the key to maintaining a crystal clear and algae-free pool lies in your commitment to regular pool care and your willingness to adapt and respond to any algae-related challenges that may arise. By staying informed and proactive, you can ensure that your pool remains a beautiful and inviting space for you, your family, and your friends to enjoy.

Chapter 7 Summary

1. Algae are microscopic, plant-like organisms that can quickly multiply and cause unsightly and potentially harmful blooms in your pool, leading to slippery surfaces, clogged filters, and poor water quality.

2. The most common types of algae found in pools are green algae, yellow or mustard algae, black algae, and pink algae (a type of bacteria).

3. Essential pool maintenance practices for algae prevention include maintaining proper water circulation, balanced water chemistry, and a clean pool environment.

4. Chemical solutions for algae control and elimination include using chlorine as a sanitizer, algaecides to target and eliminate algae, phosphate removers to starve algae from their food source, and maintaining balanced pool chemistry.

5. Non-chemical methods to combat algae growth include ensuring proper circulation and filtration, regular pool cleaning, balanced pool water, using solar pool covers.

6. Solar pool covers can help prevent algae growth by reducing the amount of sunlight that penetrates the water, as algae require sunlight to grow.

7. Staying vigilant and consistent with pool maintenance practices is crucial, as algae can quickly take over your pool if given the opportunity.

8. Maintaining a crystal clear and algae-free pool requires a commitment to regular pool care and adapting and responding to any algae-related challenges that may arise.

8. Pool Maintenance for Different Seasons

A sparkling, well-maintained pool is the centerpiece of any backyard oasis, providing endless hours of enjoyment and relaxation for family and friends. However, maintaining your pool's pristine condition requires consistent care and attention, particularly as the seasons change. Seasonal pool maintenance is essential to ensure the longevity of your pool and the safety of those who use it. This chapter will delve into the various aspects of pool maintenance for different seasons, offering practical advice and tips to help you keep your pool in tip-top shape all year round.

Each season presents unique challenges and opportunities when it comes to pool maintenance. As the weather shifts from the warmth of summer to the chill of winter, your pool's needs will also change. By understanding these seasonal variations and adapting your pool maintenance routine accordingly, you can ensure that your pool remains safe, inviting, and enjoyable for everyone.

In the following sections, we will explore the key aspects of seasonal pool maintenance, including opening and cleaning your pool for summer, maintaining pool health during the hot summer months, transitioning your pool from summer to fall, and winterizing your pool for protection and preservation. By the end of this chapter, you will have a comprehensive understanding of the steps required to maintain your pool throughout the year, allowing you to confidently adapt your pool maintenance routine for every season.

Preparing Your Pool for Summer: Opening and Cleaning

As warm summer approaches, it's time to prepare your pool for endless hours of fun and relaxation. Preparing your pool for summer involves more than just removing the cover and diving in. Proper opening and cleaning procedures are essential to ensure a safe and enjoyable swimming experience. In this section, we'll guide you through opening and cleaning your pool so that you can make the most of the sunny season.

First and foremost, gathering all the necessary tools and equipment for the job is important. You'll need a pool cover pump, a skimmer net, a pool brush, a vacuum, and the appropriate chemicals for balancing your pool water. Having these items on hand will make the process smoother and more efficient.

Begin by removing any debris, such as leaves and twigs, from the pool cover. This will prevent the debris from falling into the water when you remove the cover. Next, use a pool cover pump to remove any standing water from the cover. Once the cover is clean and dry, carefully remove it from the pool, not letting any debris fall into the water. Store the cover in a cool, dry place to prevent mold and mildew growth.

Now that the cover is off, it's time to clean the pool. Use a skimmer net to remove floating debris from the water's surface. This will make the water more inviting and help your pool's filtration system work more efficiently. Next, brush the pool walls and floor to remove dirt or algae buildup. Pay special attention to corners and crevices where algae can hide. After brushing, use a pool vacuum to remove debris from the pool floor.

Once your pool is clean, it's time to focus on the water chemistry. Test the water using a pool test kit, and adjust the chlorine, pH, alkalinity, and calcium hardness levels as needed. Proper water balance is crucial for maintaining a healthy swimming environment and preventing algae growth and equipment damage. Be sure to follow the manufacturer's instructions for your chemicals.

With your water chemistry in check, it's time to get your pool equipment up and running. Inspect your pool pump, filter, and heater for any signs of damage or wear. Clean or replace filter cartridges as needed, and lubricate any moving parts to ensure smooth operation. Turn on your pool equipment and let it run for at least twenty-four hours to circulate the water and chemicals.

Finally, inspect your pool thoroughly to ensure everything is in working order. Check for any cracks or damage to the pool's surface and repair as needed. Inspect ladders, handrails, and diving boards for stability and safety. Ensure all pool lights function properly, and replace any burnt-out bulbs.

· · ·

Maintaining Pool Health During the Hot Summer Months

As the sun shines brighter and the days grow longer, it's time to dive into the heart of pool season. The hot summer months are when your pool will see the most action, and keeping it in tip-top shape is crucial.

First and foremost, it's vital to establish a consistent cleaning routine. With increased usage and warmer temperatures, debris and algae have a higher chance of accumulating in your pool. Skim the surface daily to remove leaves, bugs, and other floating debris. Vacuum the pool floor and brush the walls at least once a week to prevent algae buildup and clear the water. Remember to clean the skimmer and pump baskets regularly, as they can become clogged with debris, hindering water circulation.

Next, let's talk about water chemistry. Balancing the chemicals in your pool is crucial for maintaining a safe and healthy swimming environment. Test the water at least twice a week, paying close attention to the pH, chlorine, and alkalinity levels. The ideal pH range is between 7.4 and 7.6, while the total alkalinity should be between 100 and 150 parts per million (ppm). As for chlorine, aim to maintain a one to three ppm level. If any of these levels are off, adjust them using the appropriate chemicals.

During the hot summer months, water evaporation occurs faster, which can lead to a decrease in water levels. Monitor your pool's water level and refill it to ensure proper skimmer and pump function. Additionally, the water loss may cause an imbalance in your pool's chemicals, so it's essential to retest and adjust them after refilling.

Another critical aspect of summer pool maintenance is the circulation system. Proper water circulation helps distribute chemicals evenly and prevents algae growth. Run your pool pump for at least eight to twelve hours a day during summer to maintain optimal circulation. Regularly check the filter and clean or replace it as needed, as a dirty filter can reduce water flow and hinder circulation.

Lastly, remember pool safety. With increased pool usage, it's essential to ensure that all safety measures are in place. Check your pool's safety equipment, such as ladders, handrails, and diving boards, for any signs of wear or damage. Inspect your pool's fencing and gates to ensure they are secure and functioning correctly. And always keep a watchful eye on swimmers, especially children, to prevent accidents.

By following these essential steps, you'll be well on your way to maintaining a healthy and inviting pool during the hot summer months. So grab your sunscreen, put on your favorite swimsuit, and dive into the refreshing waters, knowing that your pool is ready for all summer's fun and relaxation.

Transitioning Your Pool from Summer to Fall: Adjustments and Tips

As the warm summer days begin to fade and the crisp autumn air starts to settle in, adjusting your pool maintenance routine to accommodate the changing seasons is essential. Transitioning your pool from summer to fall may seem daunting, but with the right tips and tricks, you can ensure that your pool remains in pristine condition throughout the cooler months. This section will discuss the necessary adjustments and tips to help you smoothly transition your pool from summer to fall.

First and foremost, it's important to keep an eye on the weather. As temperatures begin to drop, so will the water temperature in your pool. This can affect the efficiency of your pool's equipment and the chemical balance of the water. To maintain optimal water temperature, consider investing in a pool heater or solar cover, which can help retain heat and extend your swimming season.

Next, pay close attention to the falling leaves. Autumn is notorious for shedding foliage, and these leaves can quickly accumulate in your pool, leading to clogged filters and skimmers. To prevent this, habitually skim your pool daily and empty the skimmer baskets regularly. Additionally, consider investing in a pool cover to keep leaves and debris out of the water when the pool is not used.

As the days grow shorter, adjusting your pool's circulation and filtration schedule is essential. Algae growth may slow down with less sunlight and cooler temperatures, but it's still crucial to maintain proper circulation to keep your pool water clean and clear. Adjust your pool pump's timer to run for shorter periods during the day, but ensure that it still runs long enough to circulate the entire volume of your pool at least once.

Another important aspect of transitioning your pool from summer to fall is adjusting your pool's chemical balance. Cooler water temperatures can affect the rate at which chemicals dissolve and react, so it's essential to test your pool water more frequently during this time. Pay close attention to chlorine levels, pH, alkalinity, and calcium hardness, and make any necessary adjustments to keep your pool water balanced and healthy.

Finally, remember to perform routine maintenance on your pool equipment. As you transition from summer to fall, it's a great time to inspect your pool pump, filter, heater, and other equipment for any signs of wear or damage. Clean and lubricate any moving parts, and replace any damaged components to ensure your pool equipment continues functioning efficiently throughout the fall season.

Winterizing Your Pool: Protection and Preservation

As the leaves change and the air turns crisp, it's time to start thinking about winterizing your pool. This essential process protects your pool from the harsh winter elements and preserves its components, ensuring a smooth opening come springtime. This section will guide you through the necessary steps to safeguard your pool during the colder months, so you can rest easy knowing it's well-protected.

First and foremost, it's crucial to winterize your pool before the temperature drops below freezing. This will prevent any potential damage caused by ice formation within the pool's plumbing system. To start, you'll want to balance the water chemistry, which involves adjusting the pH, alkalinity, and calcium hardness levels. This step is vital, as it helps prevent staining, scaling, and algae growth throughout winter.

Next, it's time to clean your pool thoroughly. Remove any debris, such as leaves and twigs, using a pool skimmer, and then give the pool walls and floor a good scrub with a brush. Following this, vacuum the pool to eliminate any remaining dirt and debris. Remember to clean the pool filter as well, either by backwashing or replacing the cartridge, depending on your filter type.

Once your pool is clean, you'll need to lower the water level to prevent damage from freezing water. For most pools, the water level should be lowered to approximately four to six inches below the skimmer or tile line. However, it's essential to consult your pool manufacturer's guidelines for specific recommendations. Drain any water from the pool's plumbing system, including the pump, filter, and heater, to avoid potential damage from freezing temperatures.

Now that your pool is prepped, it's time to add a winterizing algaecide and a pool enzyme product to the water. These chemicals will help prevent algae growth and break down any organic contaminants that may accumulate during winter. Follow the manufacturer's instructions for proper dosage and application.

With the water chemistry balanced and the pool clean, it's time to install a winter pool cover. This cover not only keeps debris out of your pool but also helps to prevent water evaporation and heat loss. Choose a high-quality, durable cover designed to withstand the weight of snow and ice. Secure the cover tightly, using water bags or other weights to keep it in place.

Finally, remember to store pool accessories, such as ladders, diving boards, and pool toys, in a safe and dry location. This will protect them from the elements and ensure they're ready for use when you reopen your pool in the spring.

Winterizing your pool is a crucial process that protects and preserves your investment during the colder months. Following these steps and adapting your pool maintenance routine for every season, you'll be well-prepared to enjoy a clean and healthy pool come summertime.

Adapting Your Pool Maintenance Routine for Every Season

As we reach the end of our seasonal pool maintenance journey, it is essential to emphasize the importance of adapting your pool maintenance routine to suit the ever-changing needs of each season. A well-maintained pool not only ensures the health and safety of its users but also prolongs the life of your pool equipment and structure.

Throughout this chapter, we have explored the various steps and precautions necessary to maintain a pristine pool environment, regardless of the time of year. Each season presents unique challenges and requirements, from opening and cleaning your pool in preparation for the summer months to winterizing it for protection and preservation.

In the summer, diligent pool maintenance is crucial to keep algae and bacteria at bay, ensuring crystal-clear water and a safe swimming environment. As the season transitions into fall, adjustments to your maintenance routine are necessary to accommodate the cooler temperatures and increased debris from falling leaves. Finally, winterizing your pool is vital in protecting your investment from potential damage caused by freezing temperatures and harsh weather conditions.

Adapting your pool maintenance routine for every season guarantees a clean and safe swimming environment and helps you avoid costly repairs and replacements in the long run. By following the guidelines and tips in this chapter, you can ensure that your pool remains a source of enjoyment and relaxation for you and your loved ones, regardless of the season.

In conclusion, remember that pool maintenance is an ongoing process, and staying informed about the latest techniques and best practices is essential for any pool owner. By being proactive and adapting your maintenance routine to the specific needs of each season, you can enjoy the many benefits of a well-maintained pool all year round.

Chapter 8 Summary

1. Seasonal pool maintenance is essential for ensuring your pool's longevity and its users' safety. Each season presents unique challenges and opportunities for pool care.

2. Preparing your pool for summer involves proper opening and cleaning procedures, including removing debris, cleaning the pool walls and floor, balancing water chemistry, and inspecting pool equipment.

3. During the hot summer, establish a consistent cleaning routine, maintain proper water chemistry, monitor water levels, and ensure proper circulation and filtration to keep your pool in top shape.

4. Transitioning your pool from summer to fall requires adjusting the pool's circulation and filtration schedule, maintaining proper water chemistry, and taking measures to prevent debris accumulation from falling leaves.

5. Winterizing your pool is crucial for protecting it from potential damage caused by freezing temperatures and harsh weather conditions. This process involves balancing water chemistry, cleaning the pool, lowering the water level, adding winterizing chemicals, and installing a winter pool cover.

6. Adapting your pool maintenance routine for every season guarantees a clean and safe swimming environment and helps you avoid costly repairs and replacements in the long run.

7. Regular pool maintenance, including cleaning, water chemistry management, and equipment inspection, ensures a healthy and enjoyable swimming experience for you and your loved ones.

8. Staying informed about the latest pool maintenance techniques and best practices is essential for any pool owner.

By being proactive and adapting your maintenance routine to the specific needs of each season, you can enjoy the many benefits of a well-maintained pool all year round.

9. Troubleshooting Common Pool Problems

Owning a swimming pool can be a source of endless fun and relaxation, but it also comes with its fair share of responsibilities. One of the most crucial aspects of pool ownership is ensuring that your pool remains clean, safe, and well-maintained. You will inevitably encounter various challenges and issues that require your attention and problem-solving skills. This chapter aims to provide you with the knowledge and tools necessary to address these common pool problems confidently and easily.

Troubleshooting pool problems can seem daunting, especially for new pool owners. However, with a keen eye for detail and a proactive approach, you can quickly identify and resolve most issues before they escalate into more significant concerns. The key is to familiarize yourself with the various components of your pool, understand their functions, and learn how to spot potential problems early on.

This chapter will explore some of the most common pool problems, ranging from water quality issues to structural concerns and equipment malfunctions. We will discuss practical solutions and preventative measures that you can implement to ensure your pool remains in optimal condition. By the end of this chapter, you will be well-equipped to tackle any pool-related challenge that comes your way.

As you read through the following sections, remember that every pool is unique, and the specific issues you encounter may vary depending on factors such as the type of pool, its age, and the surrounding environment. However, the fundamental principles of pool maintenance and troubleshooting remain the same. With a bit of patience and persistence, you can become a master at maintaining your pool's health and longevity.

Identifying and Addressing Water Quality Issues

Maintaining pristine water quality is the cornerstone of a healthy and enjoyable swimming pool experience. This section will discuss how to identify and address common water quality issues that can arise in your pool. By understanding the root causes and implementing practical solutions, you can ensure that your pool remains a refreshing oasis for you and your guests.

The first step in addressing water quality issues is regularly testing your pool water. This can be done using test strips or a liquid test kit, which are readily available at pool supply stores. By testing your pool water, you can monitor key parameters such as pH, total alkalinity, and sanitizer levels (chlorine or bromine). Maintaining these parameters within the recommended ranges is essential for preventing water quality problems.

One common water quality issue is cloudy or murky water. Various factors, including poor filtration, inadequate sanitizer levels, or the presence of organic contaminants, can cause this. To address cloudy water, first ensure that your pool's filtration system is functioning correctly and that the filter is clean. Next, test your sanitizer levels and adjust as necessary. If the problem persists, consider using a pool clarifier or flocculant (a substance which promotes the clumping of particles) to help remove fine particles from the water.

Another common issue is unbalanced pH and total alkalinity levels. Ideally, your pool's pH should be maintained between 7.4 and 7.6, while total alkalinity should be between 80 and 120 parts per million (ppm). Unbalanced pH can lead to skin and eye irritation and damage to pool surfaces and equipment. To correct pH and total alkalinity levels, use a pH or decreaser and alkalinity increaser as needed, following the manufacturer's instructions.

Chlorine or bromine levels that are too low can also lead to water quality issues, as they allow bacteria and other contaminants to thrive. Regularly test your sanitizer levels and adjust them to maintain the recommended range. If your sanitizer levels are consistently low, consider using a pool shock treatment to quickly raise the levels and eliminate contaminants.

In some cases, water quality issues may be caused by metals, such as iron or copper, in your pool water. This can lead to staining on pool surfaces and green or brown water. To address this issue, use a metal sequestrant to bind and remove the metals from your pool water. Additionally, ensure that your pool's pH and total alkalinity levels are properly balanced, which can help prevent metal staining.

In conclusion, identifying and addressing water quality issues is crucial to pool maintenance. By regularly testing your pool water and taking appropriate action to correct any imbalances or problems, you can ensure that your pool remains a clean, safe, and enjoyable environment for all.

Tackling Pool Surface and Structural Concerns

A sparkling, inviting pool is a joy to behold and a pleasure to swim in. However, maintaining that pristine appearance requires vigilance and a keen eye for potential problems. In this section, we'll delve into the world of the pool surface and structural concerns, offering practical advice and solutions to keep your pool in tip-top shape.

First and foremost, it's essential to understand that the pool's surface and structure are the foundation of its overall health and functionality. Issues like cracks, stains, and discoloration detract from your pool's aesthetic appeal and can lead to more severe problems if addressed. Let's explore some common surface and structural issues and how to tackle them effectively.

Stains and Discoloration

Over time, your pool's surface may develop unsightly stains or discoloration due to various factors, such as algae growth, chemical imbalances, or metal deposits. To treat these issues, start by identifying the cause of the stain. For organic stains, such as those caused by algae or leaves, a thorough scrubbing with a pool brush and proper chemical treatment should do the trick. For metal stains, you may need to use a specialized stain remover or adjust your pool's chemistry to prevent further staining.

Surface Cracks and Deterioration

Pool surfaces, especially concrete or plaster ones, are prone to cracking and deterioration over time. Small hairline cracks can be sealed with a high-quality pool caulk or sealant. However, larger cracks or significant surface deterioration may require professional resurfacing or repair. Regularly inspect your pool's surface for signs of wear and address any issues promptly to prevent more extensive damage.

Structural Damage

Structural issues, such as cracks in the pool shell or shifting of the surrounding deck, can pose serious safety hazards and lead to costly repairs if not addressed promptly. If you notice any signs of structural damage, it's crucial to consult with a pool professional to assess the situation and determine the best course of action. Repairs may be relatively simple in some cases, while in others, more extensive work may be required to ensure your pool's long-term stability and safety.

Tile and Grout Issues

Pool tiles can become loose, cracked, or discolored over time, while grout may deteriorate and allow water to seep behind the tiles. Regularly inspect your pool's tiles and grout for signs of damage and address any issues as soon as possible. Minor repairs, such as reattaching loose tiles or patching damaged grout, can often be done by the pool owner. However, more extensive tile or grout issues may require professional intervention.

Vinyl Liner Concerns

Vinyl-lined pools offer a smooth, non-porous surface that is generally low-maintenance and resistant to staining. However, vinyl liners can develop tears, punctures, or wrinkles over time. Small tears or punctures can often be repaired using a vinyl liner repair kit, while more significant issues may necessitate professional repair or liner replacement. To prevent wrinkles, ensure your pool's water level remains consistent and avoid draining the pool completely unless necessary.

Resolving Pool Equipment and Plumbing Problems

In this section, we will delve into pool equipment and plumbing problems, providing you with the knowledge and tools to tackle these issues head-on. From clogged filters to malfunctioning heaters, we will cover the most common equipment and plumbing concerns that pool owners face. By the end of this section, you will be well-equipped to handle any pool equipment or plumbing problem that comes your way.

Clogged Filters and Skimmers

A clogged filter or skimmer is one of the most common pool equipment problems. Debris, such as leaves, twigs, and insects, can accumulate in your pool's filter and skimmer baskets, obstructing water flow and reducing the efficiency of your filtration system. Regularly inspect and clean your filter and skimmer baskets to resolve this issue. If your pool water is cloudy or dirty despite regular cleaning, it may be time to replace the filter cartridge or sand.

Malfunctioning Heaters

A pool heater that needs to be fixed can be frustrating, especially when you're looking forward to a relaxing swim in warm water. Common issues with pool heaters include failure to ignite, insufficient heating, and rapid cycling on and off. To troubleshoot these problems, ensure that your heater receives adequate power and gas supply. If the issue persists, consult your heater's user manual or contact a professional.

Leaky Plumbing and Pool Shell

Leaks in your pool's plumbing system or shell can lead to water loss, increased chemical usage, and even structural damage. To identify a leak, monitor your pool's water level and observe for any wet spots or dampness around the pool area. If you suspect a leak, perform a dye test by adding a small amount near the suspected leak site and observing if the dye is drawn toward the leak. For plumbing leaks, inspect the pipes, fittings, and valves for any signs of damage or wear. If you cannot locate the leak or repair it yourself, seek the help of a professional.

Faulty Pool Pumps and Motors

A malfunctioning pool pump or motor can lead to poor water circulation, cloudy water, and algae growth. Common signs of a faulty pump or motor include unusual noises, overheating, and reduced water flow. To address these issues, check for any blockages in the pump's impeller or debris in the pump basket. If the problem persists, consult your pump's user manual or contact a pool professional for further assistance.

Automatic Pool Cleaner Issues

Automatic pool cleaners are a convenient way to keep your pool clean, but you can sometimes need help with problems. If your pool cleaner is not moving or cleaning effectively, check for any debris caught in the cleaner's gears, wheels, or tracks. Additionally, ensure that the cleaner's hose is free of kinks and that the filter bag is free of kinks. If the issue continues, consult the cleaner's user manual or contact the manufacturer for support.

Resolving pool equipment and plumbing problems is essential to maintaining a healthy and enjoyable swimming environment. By familiarizing yourself with the common issues and their solutions, you can confidently tackle these problems and keep your pool in top condition. In the next section, we will explore the management of algae and other biological infestations, further expanding your pool maintenance expertise.

Managing Algae and Other Biological Infestations

Algae and other biological infestations can quickly turn your backyard paradise into a murky, uninviting swamp. This section will explore the causes of these infestations, how to identify them, and the most effective methods for eliminating them from your pool.

Algae are microscopic plants that thrive in warm, sunlit water and can multiply rapidly if left unchecked. They come in various colors, such as green, yellow, and black, each with unique characteristics and challenges. Other biological infestations, such as bacteria and fungi, can also threaten your pool's health and the well-being of those who use it.

The first step in managing algae and other biological infestations is understanding the factors contributing to their growth. These include:

Poor water circulation: Stagnant water is an ideal breeding ground for algae and other microorganisms.

Insufficient filtration: A clogged or improperly functioning filter can allow contaminants to accumulate in your pool.

Imbalanced water chemistry: High pH levels, low sanitizer levels, and other chemical imbalances can encourage algae growth and other unwanted organisms.

To prevent and combat these infestations, consider the following strategies:

1. Regularly test and adjust your pool's water chemistry: Maintaining proper chemical balance prevents algae growth and other biological infestations. Test your pool water at least once a week and adjust the sanitizer levels, pH, alkalinity, and other essential chemicals as needed.

2. Optimize your pool's circulation and filtration systems: Ensure that your pool pump and filter are functioning correctly and are adequately sized for your pool. Regularly clean and backwash your filter to remove debris and contaminants.

3. Brush and vacuum your pool: Regularly brushing the pool walls and floor will help to dislodge algae and other microorganisms, while vacuuming will remove them from the water. This will also help to improve water circulation and filtration.

4. Shock your pool: "Shocking" your pool involves adding a large dose of sanitizer, typically chlorine, to eliminate algae and other contaminants. This should be done periodically to maintain a clean and healthy pool environment, especially after heavy use or a rainstorm.

5. Use algaecides and other specialized treatments: In some cases, it may be necessary to use algaecides or other targeted treatments to eliminate stubborn algae blooms or other biological infestations. Always follow the manufacturer's instructions and consult a pool professional if you need clarification on the best course of action.

Managing algae and other biological infestations is essential to pool maintenance. By understanding the factors contributing to their growth and implementing effective prevention and treatment strategies, you can maintain a healthy, crystal-clear pool.

. . .

Maintaining a Healthy and Problem-Free Pool

In conclusion, maintaining a healthy and problem-free pool is essential for the enjoyment of swimmers and the longevity of your pool and its equipment. By being proactive and vigilant in your pool care routine, you can prevent many common issues and ensure a safe and inviting swimming environment.

Throughout this chapter, we have explored various aspects of troubleshooting pool problems, from identifying and addressing water quality issues to tackling pool surface and structural concerns. We have also delved into resolving pool equipment and plumbing problems and managing algae and other biological infestations. By familiarizing yourself with these common pool problems and their solutions, you are well-equipped to handle any challenges that may come your way.

To maintain a healthy and problem-free pool, it is crucial to establish a regular maintenance routine that includes testing and balancing water chemistry, cleaning and inspecting pool surfaces, and ensuring the proper functioning of all pool equipment. Additionally, it is essential to stay informed about new pool care products and techniques and consult with pool professionals when necessary.

By taking a proactive approach to pool maintenance, you can save time, money, and frustration in the long run. A well-maintained pool provides a safe and enjoyable swimming experience and contributes to the overall aesthetic appeal of your outdoor living space. With the knowledge and skills acquired in this chapter, you are now better prepared to tackle any pool problems and maintain a pristine and inviting swimming environment for years to come.

Remember, a healthy and problem-free pool is not a luxury but an attainable goal that can be achieved with dedication, knowledge, and a little elbow grease. So, dive in and enjoy the crystal-clear waters of your well-maintained pool, knowing you have the tools and expertise to keep it in top-notch condition.

Chapter 9 Summary

1. Regularly testing and adjusting your pool's water chemistry is crucial for maintaining water quality and preventing issues such as cloudy water, unbalanced pH, and low sanitizer levels.

2. Addressing pool surfaces and structural concerns, such as stains, cracks, and tile or grout issues, is essential for maintaining the pool's aesthetic appeal and preventing more severe problems.

3. Resolving pool equipment and plumbing problems, such as clogged filters, malfunctioning heaters, and leaky pipes, is vital for maintaining a healthy and enjoyable swimming environment.

4. Managing algae and other biological infestations involves understanding the factors contributing to their growth and implementing effective prevention and treatment strategies, such as optimizing water circulation, filtration, and chemical balance.

5. Establishing a regular maintenance routine that includes testing and balancing water chemistry, cleaning and inspecting pool surfaces, and ensuring the proper functioning of all pool equipment is vital to maintaining a healthy and problem-free pool.

6. Being proactive and vigilant in your pool care routine can prevent many common issues and ensure a safe and inviting swimming environment for all.

7. Staying informed about new pool care products and techniques and consulting with pool professionals when necessary can help you tackle any pool-related challenges that may come your way.

10. Pool Safety and Regulations

Swimming pools are a source of endless fun, relaxation, and exercise for people of all ages. However, with the enjoyment they bring, it's crucial to remember the importance of maintaining a safe and secure environment for everyone. Pool safety and adherence to regulations are essential aspects of pool ownership that cannot be overlooked. In this chapter, we will explore the various facets of pool safety and regulations, ensuring you have the knowledge and tools to create a secure swimming haven for all.

The importance of pool safety and regulations cannot be overstated. According to the Centers for Disease Control and Prevention (CDC), drowning is the leading cause of unintentional injury-related death for children aged one to four. Furthermore, for every child who dies from drowning, another five receive emergency care for nonfatal submersion injuries. These alarming statistics highlight the need for stringent safety measures and adherence to regulations in and around swimming pools.

In this chapter, we will delve into the various aspects of pool safety, including understanding local and national pool regulations, implementing safety measures for swimmers, ensuring proper maintenance for a safe pool environment, and educating pool users on safety guidelines and best practices. By the end of this chapter, you will have a comprehensive understanding of the importance of pool safety and how to maintain a secure environment for all who enjoy your pool.

As a responsible pool owner, you must ensure your pool is safe for everyone. This involves following the necessary regulations and creating a culture of safety awareness among all pool users. By educating yourself and others on the importance of pool safety and regulations, you are taking a vital step toward preventing accidents and ensuring that your pool remains a source of joy and entertainment for years to come.

Understanding Local and National Pool Regulations

Pool safety is a critical aspect of pool maintenance, and adhering to local and national pool regulations is essential for maintaining a safe and enjoyable swimming environment. These regulations are designed to protect swimmers and pool owners, ensuring everyone can enjoy the benefits of a well-maintained pool without the risk of accidents or health hazards. In this section, we will explore the importance of understanding and following local and national pool regulations and how to stay informed about any changes or updates to these rules.

Local pool regulations can vary significantly depending on your location, so you must familiarize yourself with the specific rules and guidelines that apply to your area. These regulations may cover many topics, including pool construction, water quality, safety equipment, and operational procedures. Some standard local regulations may include requirements for fencing and barriers, pool depth markers, and the presence of life-saving equipment such as life rings and rescue poles.

In addition to local regulations, national pool safety standards apply to pools across the country. In the United States, for example, the Centers for Disease Control and Prevention (CDC) has established the Model Aquatic Health Code (MAHC), which guides various aspects of pool safety and maintenance. The MAHC covers water quality, facility design, lifeguarding, and risk management, among others. While the MAHC is not legally binding, many states and local jurisdictions have adopted its recommendations as part of their pool regulations.

To ensure that you comply with local and national pool regulations, you must stay informed about any changes or updates to these rules. This can be accomplished by regularly checking your local government's websites and relevant national organizations, such as the CDC or the Association of Pool and Spa Professionals (APSP).

Understanding and adhering to local and national pool regulations can help create a safe and enjoyable swimming environment for everyone who uses your pool. Not only will this protect swimmers from potential hazards, but it can also protect you as a pool owner from potential liability issues. In the next section, we will discuss specific pool safety measures that can be implemented to further enhance the safety of your pool for all swimmers.

Implementing Pool Safety Measures for Swimmers

Pool safety is of paramount importance, as it ensures the well-being of swimmers and prevents accidents from occurring. In this section, we will discuss various safety measures that can be implemented to create a secure environment for swimmers of all ages and skill levels. Adhering to these guidelines can provide everyone with a safe and enjoyable swimming experience.

1. Establish and enforce pool rules: Display pool rules and regulations in a prominent location, ensuring that all swimmers know the expectations. Standard rules include no running and no diving in shallow areas. Encourage swimmers to follow these rules and enforce them consistently to maintain a safe environment.

2. Provide appropriate safety equipment: Equip your pool with essential safety gear, such as life jackets, floatation devices, and rescue equipment, like life rings and reaching poles. Ensure that these items are easily accessible and in good working condition. Additionally, consider installing slip-resistant surfaces around the pool area to prevent falls.

3. Implement a buddy system: Encourage swimmers to swim continuously with a buddy, especially for children and inexperienced swimmers. This system ensures that someone is always watching out for each swimmer, providing an extra layer of safety.

4. Offer swimming lessons: Providing swimming lessons for beginners can significantly reduce the risk of accidents. Teaching proper swimming techniques and water safety skills empowers swimmers to feel confident and secure in the water.

5. Regularly inspect pool barriers and fencing: Ensure your pool is surrounded by a secure barrier or fence meeting local regulations. Regularly inspect the barrier for any damage or wear and promptly address any issues to prevent unauthorized access, especially by young children.

6. Maintain water quality: Regularly test and adjust the pool's water chemistry to ensure it is safe for swimming. Proper water balance helps prevent the growth of harmful bacteria and algae, which can cause illness or injury to swimmers.

7. Encourage proper hygiene: Encourage swimmers to shower before entering the pool and to avoid swimming if they are ill or have open wounds. This helps maintain water quality and prevents the spread of germs.

8. Create an emergency action plan: Develop a comprehensive action plan that outlines the steps to take in an accident or medical emergency. Ensure all family members are familiar with the plan and know how to respond appropriately.

By implementing these pool safety measures, you can create a secure and enjoyable swimming environment for all users. Remember, a safe pool is a happy pool, and by prioritizing the well-being of your swimmers, you contribute to a positive and rewarding experience for everyone involved.

Ensuring Proper Maintenance for a Safe Pool Environment

A well-maintained pool is not only visually appealing but also plays a crucial role in ensuring the safety and well-being of its users. This section will delve into the importance of proper pool maintenance and the steps you can take to create a safe and enjoyable environment for swimmers.

First and foremost, maintaining the water quality in your pool is essential for a safe swimming experience. This involves regularly testing and adjusting the water's pH, alkalinity, and sanitizer levels to keep them within the recommended ranges. A balanced pool environment prevents the growth of harmful bacteria and algae and reduces the risk of skin irritation and other health issues for swimmers. Additionally, keep the pool water clean and clear by removing debris, such as leaves and dirt, and regularly vacuuming the pool floor.

Another critical aspect of pool maintenance is ensuring the proper functioning of the pool's circulation system. A well-functioning circulation system, which includes the pump, filter, and skimmer, helps distribute chemicals evenly throughout the pool and removes contaminants. Regularly inspect and clean the skimmer baskets, filter cartridges, and pool pump to prevent clogs and ensure optimal performance.

The pool's surrounding area also plays a significant role in maintaining a safe environment. Regularly clean and inspect the pool deck, ladders, diving boards, and other pool accessories to ensure they are in good condition and free from hazards. Repair or replace any damaged or worn-out equipment to prevent accidents and injuries. Additionally, keep the pool deck clear of obstacles and slippery surfaces by promptly removing water puddles and using non-slip materials for the deck flooring.

Proper pool maintenance also includes addressing any electrical hazards that may pose a risk to swimmers. Ensure that all electrical components, such as underwater lights, pool pumps, and heaters, are correctly installed and grounded. Schedule regular inspections by a licensed electrician to verify the safety of your pool's electrical system and address any potential issues.

Lastly, it is essential to have a well-maintained safety equipment inventory on hand. This includes life rings, rescue poles, first aid kits, and pool signage that displays safety rules and guidelines. Regularly inspect and replace safety equipment as needed to ensure they are in good working condition and readily available in an emergency.

Proper pool maintenance is vital to creating a safe and enjoyable swimming environment. By diligently addressing water quality, circulation systems, pool accessories, electrical components, and safety equipment, you can ensure that your pool remains secure and inviting for all users.

Educating Pool Users on Safety Guidelines and Best Practices

The key to maintaining a safe and enjoyable pool environment lies not only in the hands of the pool owner or operator but also in the awareness and cooperation of the pool users. Educating swimmers on safety guidelines and best practices is essential to pool safety and can significantly reduce the risk of accidents and injuries. This section will explore various methods and strategies for effectively communicating pool safety information to users, ensuring that everyone can enjoy the water with confidence and peace of mind.

One of the most effective ways to educate pool users on safety guidelines is by providing clear and concise information. This can be achieved through signage. Signs should be prominently displayed around the pool area, outlining essential safety rules such as no diving in shallow areas, no running on the pool deck, and the importance of adult supervision for young swimmers.

Another important aspect of educating pool users on safety guidelines is fostering a culture of open communication and feedback. Encourage swimmers to report any potential hazards or safety concerns they may encounter and be proactive in addressing these issues. By involving users in maintaining a safe pool environment, you can empower them to take ownership of their safety and the safety of others.

It is also essential to educate pool users on the importance of personal responsibility regarding pool safety. This includes understanding their swimming abilities and limitations and being aware of the potential risks associated with certain activities or behaviors. Encourage swimmers to take swimming lessons if they need more confidence in their abilities, and remind them to swim continuously with a buddy.

Educating pool users on safety guidelines and best practices is crucial to maintaining a safe and enjoyable swimming environment. By providing clear information, encouraging open communication, and fostering a culture of shared responsibility, pool operators can ensure that everyone can enjoy the water with confidence and peace of mind.

The Importance of Pool Safety and Adhering to Regulations

In conclusion, the significance of pool safety and adhering to regulations cannot be overstated. As a pool owner or operator, you must ensure that the aquatic environment is safe and enjoyable for all users. By understanding and implementing local and national pool regulations, you are protecting swimmers from potential hazards and safeguarding yourself from any legal liabilities.

Throughout this chapter, we have explored various aspects of pool safety, from understanding the rules and regulations to implementing safety measures for swimmers. By ensuring proper maintenance of your pool environment, you are creating a space where people can enjoy the water without fear of accidents or injuries. Furthermore, educating pool users on safety guidelines and best practices is essential for fostering a culture of awareness and responsibility.

In summary, pool safety and regulations are integral to maintaining a successful and enjoyable aquatic environment. By staying informed and proactive in your approach to pool safety, you can create a space where swimmers can enjoy the water with peace of mind. Remember, a safe pool is a happy pool, and your commitment to safety will ultimately lead to a more enjoyable experience for everyone involved.

Chapter 10 Summary

1. Pool safety and adherence to regulations are crucial aspects of pool ownership, as they ensure a secure and enjoyable environment for all users.

2. Understanding and following local and national pool regulations is essential for maintaining a safe swimming environment and protecting swimmers and pool owners from potential hazards and liabilities.

3. Implementing pool safety measures, such as establishing and enforcing pool rules, and providing appropriate safety equipment can significantly reduce the risk of accidents and injuries.

4. Proper pool maintenance, including maintaining water quality, ensuring the proper functioning of the circulation system, and addressing electrical hazards, plays a vital role in creating a safe and enjoyable swimming environment.

5. Educating pool users on safety guidelines and best practices is essential for fostering a culture of awareness and responsibility among swimmers.

6. Open communication and feedback between pool operators and users can help identify potential hazards and safety concerns, leading to a safer pool environment.

11. Energy Efficiency and Eco-friendly Pool Practices

Welcome to the world of energy efficiency and eco-friendly pool practices! As a pool owner, you have the unique opportunity to positively impact the environment while saving money on your energy bills. In this chapter, we will explore various ways to create a more sustainable and energy-efficient pool environment without sacrificing the enjoyment and relaxation that your pool provides.

The importance of energy efficiency and eco-friendly practices has grown significantly in recent years as more and more people recognize the need to conserve resources and reduce their carbon footprint. This shift in mindset has led to the development of innovative technologies and practices that can help pool owners maintain their pools in a more environmentally friendly manner.

By adopting energy-efficient pool equipment, implementing solar power for heating and lighting, conserving water, and using eco-friendly cleaning and maintenance techniques, you can create a pool that is enjoyable and kind to the planet. In doing so, you'll contribute to a greener future for generations.

In the following sections, we will delve into the specifics of these eco-friendly pool practices, providing practical tips and guidance on making your pool more energy-efficient and environmentally friendly. So, let's dive in and start making a difference today!

Choosing Energy-Efficient Pool Equipment

As a pool owner, you have a unique opportunity to positively impact the environment by selecting energy-efficient pool equipment. In this section, we will explore various energy-efficient pool equipment options and offer guidance on how to make the best choices for your pool.

Energy-Efficient Pool Pumps

The pool pump is the heart of your pool's circulation system, responsible for moving water through the filter and ensuring the proper distribution of chemicals. Traditional pool pumps, however, can consume a significant amount of energy. To reduce energy consumption, consider investing in a variable-speed or two-speed pump. These pumps allow you to adjust the speed and flow rate according to your pool's needs, resulting in up to 70% energy savings. Additionally, look for pumps with an ENERGY STAR certification, which ensures they meet strict energy efficiency guidelines set by the US Environmental Protection Agency.

Energy-Efficient Pool Filters

Your pool filter is crucial in keeping your pool water clean and clear. There are three main types of pool filters: sand, cartridge, and diatomaceous earth (DE). While each type has pros and cons, cartridge filters are generally considered the most energy-efficient option. They require less water for backwashing, which reduces the energy needed to pump water through the filter. Moreover, cartridge filters can effectively capture debris without requiring a high water flow rate, allowing you to run your pool pump at a lower speed and save energy.

LED Pool Lighting

Traditional incandescent and halogen pool lights can be energy hogs, consuming significant electricity. Switching to LED pool lights can drastically reduce your pool's energy consumption, as they use up to 80% less energy than their traditional counterparts. LED lights also have a longer lifespan, meaning fewer replacements and less waste. They also come in various colors and styles, allowing you to create a visually appealing and energy-efficient pool environment.

Energy-Efficient Pool Heaters

Heating your pool can be one of the most energy-intensive aspects of pool ownership. To minimize energy consumption, consider investing in an energy-efficient pool heater. Solar pool heaters, for example, harness the sun's power to heat your pool water, resulting in zero emissions and minimal operating costs. Alternatively, heat pumps and gas heaters with high energy efficiency ratings can also help reduce your pool's energy consumption while maintaining a comfortable water temperature.

Choosing energy-efficient pool equipment is essential to creating a more eco-friendly and cost-effective pool environment. By selecting ENERGY STAR-certified pumps, cartridge filters, LED lighting, and energy-efficient heaters, you can significantly reduce your pool's energy consumption while still enjoying all the benefits of pool ownership. Remember, every small step towards energy efficiency counts and contributes to a greener, more sustainable future for our planet.

Implementing Solar Power for Pool Heating and Lighting

Harnessing the sun's power is one of the most effective ways to make your pool more energy-efficient and eco-friendly. In this section, we will explore the benefits of using solar power for pool heating and lighting and provide practical tips on implementing this sustainable solution.

Solar Pool Heating

Solar pool heating systems are an excellent option for those looking to reduce their reliance on traditional energy sources and decrease their pool's environmental impact. These systems utilize solar collectors, typically installed on the roof or a nearby structure, to absorb sunlight and convert it into heat. The heated water is then circulated back into the pool, maintaining a comfortable temperature without gas or electric heaters.

There are several advantages to using solar pool heating systems, including:

- Cost savings: While the initial investment for a solar pool heating system may be higher than traditional heaters, the long-term savings on energy bills can be significant. Solar pool heaters have minimal operating costs and can last up to twenty years with proper maintenance, making them a cost-effective choice in the long run.

- Reduced emissions: Solar pool heating systems produce no greenhouse gas emissions, making them an environmentally friendly alternative to gas and electric heaters.

- Low maintenance: Solar pool heating systems have fewer moving parts than traditional heaters, which means less maintenance and fewer repairs.

Solar Pool Lighting

In addition to heating your pool, solar power can also be used to illuminate your pool area, making it safer and more enjoyable for nighttime swimming. Solar pool lights are available in various styles, including floating lights, underwater lights, and deck-mounted lights. These lights are powered by solar panels that charge during the day and automatically turn on at night, providing a sustainable and energy-efficient lighting solution.

Some benefits of using solar pool lighting include the following:

- Energy savings: Solar pool lights require no electricity to operate, so you'll save on energy costs and reduce your pool's overall energy consumption.

- Easy installation: Solar pool lights are generally easy, with no wiring or electrical work required. This makes them an ideal choice for both new pool installations and existing pools looking to upgrade their lighting systems.

- Low maintenance: Solar pool lights have a long lifespan and require minimal maintenance, making them a hassle-free lighting solution for your pool area.

Implementing solar power for pool heating and lighting is a smart and sustainable choice for pool owners looking to reduce their environmental impact and save on energy costs. Investing in solar pool heating systems and lights lets you enjoy a comfortable, well-lit pool area while embracing a greener pool lifestyle.

. . .

Water Conservation Techniques for Your Pool

Water conservation is a crucial aspect of maintaining an eco-friendly pool. Not only does it help you save money on your water bill, but it also contributes to preserving our planet's most precious resource. This section will explore various water conservation techniques you can implement in your pool to create a more sustainable and environmentally friendly swimming experience.

Regularly Check for Leaks

One of the most effective ways to conserve water in your pool is by regularly checking for leaks. A small leak can lead to significant water loss over time, so addressing any issues as soon as they arise is essential. Inspect your pool's plumbing, pumps, and filters for any signs of leaks, and repair them promptly. Additionally, keep an eye on your water bill for any sudden spikes in usage, which could indicate a hidden leak.

Use a Pool Cover

A pool cover is an excellent investment for water conservation. Not only does it prevent water evaporation, but it also helps maintain the pool's temperature, reducing the need for additional heating. Using a pool cover can save up to 50% of your pool's water loss due to evaporation. Furthermore, a pool cover removes debris from the water, reducing the need for constant cleaning and refilling.

Optimize Backwashing

Backwashing your pool's filter is necessary to keep it clean and functioning correctly. However, excessive backwashing can lead to significant water waste. To conserve water, only backwash your pool when the pressure gauge indicates it's necessary, typically when it reaches eight to ten psi above the starting pressure. Additionally, consider upgrading to a high-efficiency filter that requires less frequent backwashing.

Install a Rainwater Harvesting System

Collecting rainwater is an eco-friendly and cost-effective way to replenish your pool's water supply. By installing a rainwater harvesting system, you can capture and store rainwater for topping off your pool or even watering your garden. This practice conserves water and reduces the demand for local water sources.

Practice Smart Pool Filling

When it's time to fill your pool, be mindful of your water usage. Use a hose timer to prevent overfilling and wasting water. Additionally, consider filling your pool during the cooler hours of the day or at night to minimize evaporation.

Educate Pool Users

Finally, educate your family and guests on the importance of water conservation. Encourage them to practice water-saving habits, such as taking shorter showers before entering the pool and not splashing water out during play. By fostering a culture of water conservation, you can ensure that your pool remains eco-friendly for years to come.

By implementing these water conservation techniques, you can significantly reduce your pool's environmental impact while saving money on your water bill. Embracing these eco-friendly practices will benefit your pool and contribute to a more sustainable future for our planet.

Eco-friendly Pool Cleaning and Maintenance

In this section, we will delve into eco-friendly pool cleaning and maintenance, a crucial aspect of embracing a greener pool lifestyle. By adopting environmentally friendly practices in your pool care routine, you contribute to our planet's well-being and ensure a healthier swimming environment for you and your loved ones.

Natural Pool Chemicals

Traditional pool chemicals, such as chlorine and bromine, can harm the environment and may cause skin and eye irritation for swimmers. As a more sustainable alternative, consider using natural pool chemicals derived from plant and mineral sources. These eco-friendly options are biodegradable, non-toxic, and gentle on the environment and your skin. Some popular natural pool chemicals include enzymes, mineral sanitizers, and saltwater systems. By making the switch, you can maintain a clean and safe pool without the harsh side effects of traditional chemicals.

Pool Skimming and Vacuuming

Regular pool skimming and vacuuming are essential for maintaining a clean, debris-free swimming environment. However, manual pool cleaning can be time-consuming and labor-intensive. To reduce energy consumption and make pool maintenance more efficient, consider investing in an energy-efficient pool cleaner, such as a robotic pool vacuum. These devices are designed to consume less energy while providing thorough and effective cleaning. Additionally, they can help reduce the need for chemical treatments by removing debris and contaminants before they can affect your pool's water quality.

Eco-friendly Pool Filters

Your pool filter is vital in keeping your pool water clean and clear. Traditional sand filters can consume a significant amount of water during the backwashing process, which can be wasteful and harmful to the environment. Consider using a cartridge filter or a diatomaceous earth (DE) filter as an eco-friendly alternative. These filters require less water for cleaning and maintenance and are more effective at trapping smaller particles, resulting in cleaner and more transparent pool water.

Regular Maintenance Checks

One of the most effective ways to maintain an eco-friendly pool is by conducting regular maintenance checks. This includes inspecting your pool equipment for any signs of wear and tear, checking for leaks, and monitoring your pool's water chemistry. By addressing any issues promptly, you can prevent more significant problems down the line and reduce the need for chemical treatments and excessive energy consumption. Regular maintenance checks also ensure that your pool equipment runs efficiently, which can help prolong its lifespan and reduce your overall environmental impact.

Adopting eco-friendly pool cleaning and maintenance practices is vital to embracing a greener pool lifestyle. By choosing natural pool chemicals, investing in energy-efficient pool equipment, and conducting regular maintenance checks, you can create a healthier and more sustainable swimming environment. Not only will these practices benefit the environment, but they will also contribute to a more enjoyable and cost-effective pool ownership experience.

Embracing a Greener Pool Lifestyle

As we reach the end of this enlightening journey, we must reflect on the importance of adopting energy-efficient and eco-friendly practices for our pools. Not only do these practices contribute to a healthier environment, but they also help in reducing our carbon footprint and save energy costs. By embracing a greener pool lifestyle, we can ensure that our love for swimming and poolside relaxation does not come at the expense of our planet's well-being.

This chapter has explored various methods to make your pool more energy-efficient and eco-friendly. From selecting energy-efficient pool equipment to harnessing the sun's power for heating and lighting, there are numerous ways to create a sustainable pool environment. Additionally, we have discussed water conservation techniques and eco-friendly cleaning and maintenance practices that can significantly reduce the environmental impact of your pool.

As a responsible pool owner, it is crucial to stay informed and continually seek ways to improve the sustainability of your pool. By doing so, you can enjoy the benefits of a cleaner, more efficient pool while contributing to a healthier planet for future generations.

In conclusion, adopting energy-efficient and eco-friendly pool practices is a smart decision for the environment and your wallet. You can create an enjoyable and sustainable pool by implementing the strategies discussed in this chapter.

Chapter 11 Summary

1. Energy-efficient and eco-friendly pool practices are essential for reducing environmental impact, conserving resources, and saving on energy costs.

2. Choosing energy-efficient pool equipment, such as variable-speed pumps, cartridge filters, LED lighting, and energy-efficient heaters, can significantly reduce energy consumption.

3. Implementing solar power for pool heating and lighting is a sustainable and cost-effective solution that harnesses renewable energy and reduces carbon emissions.

4. Water conservation techniques, such as regularly checking for leaks, using a pool cover, optimizing backwashing, and installing a rainwater harvesting system, can help preserve water resources and save on water bills.

5. Eco-friendly pool cleaning and maintenance practices, including using natural pool chemicals, investing in energy-efficient pool cleaners, and conducting regular maintenance checks, contribute to a healthier swimming environment and reduce environmental impact.

6. Educating pool users on the importance of water conservation and eco-friendly practices can foster a culture of sustainability and responsible pool ownership.

7. Regular maintenance checks ensure that pool equipment runs efficiently, prolonging its lifespan and reducing overall environmental impact.

8. Embracing a greener pool lifestyle benefits the environment and contributes to a more enjoyable and cost-effective pool ownership experience.

12. Enjoying a Well-Maintained Pool

A shimmering, crystal-clear pool is the epitome of luxury and relaxation. It's a place to unwind, have fun, and create lasting memories with family and friends. However, maintaining a pool behind the scenes requires consistent care and attention. This final chapter will explore the numerous rewards of diligent pool maintenance and how it can enhance your overall poolside experience.

Consistent pool care is not just about keeping the water clean and free of debris; it's about ensuring the longevity of your investment and creating a safe, healthy environment for everyone to enjoy. A well-maintained pool is a source of pride and satisfaction and can significantly improve your life quality.

Throughout this book, we have delved into the various aspects of pool maintenance, from understanding the chemistry of your pool water to mastering the art of skimming and vacuuming. We have also discussed the importance of regular equipment checks and the benefits of timely repairs. Now, it's time to bring it all together and appreciate the fruits of your labor.

In this chapter, we will discuss the impact of regular maintenance on your pool's longevity, the health benefits of a clean and safe swimming environment, and how proper upkeep can enhance your overall poolside experience. We will also touch upon the financial advantages of preventative pool maintenance and conclude with some final thoughts on embracing the joy of a pristine pool.

So, let's dive in, celebrate the rewards of consistent pool care, and learn how to make the most of your beautiful, well-maintained pool.

The Impact of Regular Maintenance on Pool Longevity

A well-maintained pool is a delight to swim in and a valuable asset that can last for many years. Like any other significant investment, your swimming pool requires consistent care and attention to ensure longevity. In this section, we will explore the impact of regular maintenance on the lifespan of your pool and discuss the importance of establishing a routine that keeps your pool in pristine condition.

To begin with, it is essential to understand that pools are complex systems with numerous components working together to create a safe and enjoyable environment. These components include the pool's structure, filtration system, water chemistry, and various accessories. Each of these elements plays a crucial role in your pool's overall performance and longevity. Dedicating time and effort to regular maintenance can prevent minor issues from escalating into costly repairs or even irreversible damage.

One of the most critical aspects of pool maintenance is ensuring that the water remains clean and chemically balanced. This involves regularly testing the water for pH, chlorine, and other essential levels and adjusting them as needed. By doing so, you can prevent the growth of harmful bacteria and algae, which can cause damage to your pool's surfaces and equipment. Furthermore, balanced water chemistry helps maintain your pool's structural integrity, preventing issues such as corrosion and staining.

Another vital aspect of pool maintenance is the upkeep of the filtration system. A well-functioning filter is crucial for removing debris and contaminants from the water, ensuring it remains clean and clear. Regularly cleaning or replacing filter cartridges, backwashing sand filters, and inspecting the filtration system's overall condition will help prolong its lifespan and maintain optimal performance.

In addition to water chemistry and filtration, regular maintenance should include the inspection and upkeep of your pool's physical structure. This involves checking for cracks, leaks, or other signs of wear and tear and promptly addressing any necessary repairs. By doing so, you can prevent further damage and extend the life of your pool.

Lastly, the proper care and storage of pool accessories, such as covers, ladders, and cleaning equipment, can also contribute to the longevity of your pool. Ensuring that these items are in good condition and used correctly prevents damage to your pool's surfaces and maintains a safe swimming environment.

The impact of regular maintenance on pool longevity cannot be overstated. By establishing a consistent routine that addresses all aspects of pool care, you can enjoy the numerous benefits of a well-maintained pool for years to come. This will enhance your poolside experience and protect your investment and ensure that your pool remains a source of joy and relaxation for you and your loved ones.

Health Benefits of a Clean and Safe Swimming Environment

A well-maintained pool looks inviting and offers numerous health benefits to swimmers. By consistently caring for your pool, you ensure a clean and safe environment for you and your loved ones. This section will explore the various health advantages of a pristine swimming environment, highlighting the importance of regular pool maintenance.

First and foremost, a clean pool helps prevent the spread of waterborne illnesses. Bacteria, viruses, and other pathogens can thrive in poorly maintained pools, leading to infections and diseases such as swimmer's ear, gastrointestinal issues, and skin rashes. By diligently maintaining your pool's water chemistry, you can effectively neutralize these harmful microorganisms, safeguarding the health of everyone who takes a dip.

In addition to reducing the risk of illness, a well-maintained pool promotes physical fitness. Swimming is a low-impact, full-body workout that can improve cardiovascular health, increase muscle strength, and enhance flexibility. With a clean and safe swimming environment, you and your family will be more inclined to engage in this enjoyable form of exercise regularly. Moreover, swimming can also help alleviate stress and improve mental well-being, making pool maintenance an investment in your overall health.

Another health benefit of a clean pool is the prevention of pool-related accidents. Slippery surfaces caused by algae growth can lead to falls and injuries, while improperly balanced water can cause eye and skin irritation. Keeping your pool clean and well-maintained minimizes these risks and creates a safer environment for swimmers of all ages.

Furthermore, a well-maintained pool can improve air quality around your area. Properly functioning pool equipment, such as filters and pumps, helps remove contaminants and debris from the water, preventing the release of harmful substances into the air. This results in a fresher, more pleasant atmosphere for you and your guests.

The health benefits of a clean and safe swimming environment are numerous and far-reaching. By investing time and effort into regular pool maintenance, you are enhancing the aesthetic appeal of your pool and promoting the well-being of everyone who uses it.

Enhancing Your Poolside Experience with Proper Upkeep

A well-maintained pool is not just about ensuring its longevity and safety but also about elevating your overall poolside experience. Investing time and effort into proper pool upkeep creates a more enjoyable and inviting environment for yourself, your family, and your guests. In this section, we will explore how consistent pool care can enhance your poolside experience.

First and foremost, a clean and sparkling pool is visually appealing. Crystal-clear water, free of debris and algae, invites swimmers to dive in and enjoy the refreshing embrace of the water. A pool that is well cared for also exudes a sense of pride and accomplishment, reflecting the dedication and attention to detail that you, as the pool owner, have invested in its maintenance.

In addition to the visual appeal, a well-maintained pool also contributes to a more pleasant and relaxing atmosphere. When your pool equipment functions efficiently, and the water chemistry is balanced, you can enjoy the soothing sounds of water flowing through the filtration system and the gentle lapping of waves against the pool walls. This tranquil ambiance creates the perfect backdrop for unwinding after a long day or spending quality time with loved ones.

Proper pool upkeep also ensures that your poolside amenities and features are in optimal working condition. This includes everything from your pool's lighting system to heating and circulation components. Regularly inspecting and maintaining these elements guarantees a comfortable and enjoyable swimming experience, regardless of the time of day or the season.

Another aspect of enhancing your poolside experience through proper maintenance is the prevention of unpleasant odors and irritations. A well-balanced pool, free of bacteria and algae, will not emit any foul smells and will not cause skin or eye irritations for swimmers. This allows you and your guests to enjoy your time in and around the pool without discomfort or distractions.

Lastly, a well-maintained pool can be the perfect setting for social gatherings and special occasions. Whether hosting a casual weekend barbecue or celebrating a milestone event, your pristine pool will undoubtedly be the centerpiece of the festivities. By ensuring that your pool is always in top condition, you can create lasting memories with friends and family in a beautiful, inviting environment.

Proper pool upkeep not only extends the life of your pool and promotes a safe swimming environment, but it also significantly enhances your overall poolside experience. By dedicating yourself to consistent pool care, you can enjoy the countless benefits and pleasures of owning a clean, safe, and visually stunning pool.

The Financial Advantages of Preventative Pool Maintenance

Investing time and effort into preventative pool maintenance can save money in the long run and ensure that your pool remains an enjoyable and valuable asset.

One of the primary financial benefits of regular pool care is the prevention of costly repairs. Neglected pools are more susceptible to algae growth, damaged equipment, and imbalanced water chemistry. These problems can lead to expensive repairs or even the need for complete pool resurfacing. By adhering to a consistent maintenance routine, you can identify and address minor issues before they escalate into major, costly concerns.

Another financial advantage of preventative pool maintenance is the extended lifespan of your pool equipment. Filters, pumps, and heaters are essential components of your pool system, and their proper functioning is crucial for maintaining a clean and safe swimming environment. Regular cleaning, inspection, and replacement of worn-out parts can significantly prolong the life of your equipment, saving you money on replacements and ensuring optimal performance.

Energy efficiency is another area where preventative pool maintenance can lead to financial savings. A clean, well-maintained pool requires less energy to circulate water and maintain the desired temperature. By keeping your pool free of debris, ensuring the water chemistry is balanced, and regularly servicing your pool equipment, you can reduce energy consumption and lower utility bills.

Moreover, a well-maintained pool can enhance the overall value of your property. Prospective homebuyers are often attracted to homes with pristine pools, as they signify a well-cared-for property and offer an appealing outdoor living space. By investing in regular pool maintenance, you can preserve and increase your property's value, making it more attractive to potential buyers.

The financial advantages of preventative pool maintenance are numerous and significant. By dedicating time and effort to regular pool care, you can prevent costly repairs, extend the life of your equipment, reduce energy consumption, and boost your property's value. Ultimately, a well-maintained pool is a source of enjoyment and a wise financial investment.

Embracing the Joy of a Pristine Pool

As we reach the end of this comprehensive guide on pool maintenance, it's time to take a step back and truly appreciate the beauty and joy that a pristine pool can bring into our lives. A well-maintained pool is not just a luxury but a testament to the dedication and care you've invested in creating a safe, clean, and enjoyable space for yourself, your family, and your friends.

The journey of pool maintenance may have seemed daunting at first, but by now, you should feel confident in your ability to tackle any challenge that comes your way. With the knowledge and skills you've acquired, you are now well-equipped to handle the various aspects of pool care, from maintaining the perfect water balance to ensuring the efficiency of your pool equipment.

The rewards of consistent pool care are truly invaluable. A well-maintained pool enhances your investment's longevity and contributes to a healthier swimming environment. By keeping your pool clean and safe, you are promoting the well-being of everyone who takes a dip in its refreshing waters.

Moreover, a pristine pool can significantly elevate your poolside experience. Imagine lounging by the crystal-clear water, basking in the sun, and enjoying the gentle lapping of the water against the pool's edge. These moments of relaxation and leisure are all the more enjoyable when your pool is in its best condition.

In addition, the financial advantages of preventative pool maintenance must be balanced. Taking care of your pool and addressing potential issues before they escalate saves you from costly repairs and replacements in the long run. This proactive approach protects your wallet and ensures that your pool remains a source of joy and relaxation for years to come.

In conclusion, embracing the joy of a pristine pool is a rewarding endeavor that enriches your life and the lives of those around you. By committing to consistent pool care and maintenance, you invest in a happier, healthier, and more enjoyable future.

Chapter 12 Summary

1. Consistent pool care is essential for maintaining a clean, safe, and enjoyable swimming environment and ensuring your investment's longevity.

2. Regular maintenance, including water chemistry balance, filtration system upkeep, and structural inspections, can prevent minor issues from escalating into costly repairs or irreversible damage.

3. A well-maintained pool offers numerous health benefits, such as preventing waterborne illnesses, promoting physical fitness, and creating a safer environment for swimmers.

4. Proper pool upkeep enhances the overall poolside experience by creating a visually appealing, relaxing atmosphere and ensuring optimal pool amenities and features functioning.

5. Preventative pool maintenance offers financial advantages, including preventing costly repairs, extending the lifespan of pool equipment, reducing energy consumption, and increasing property value.

6. A pristine pool provides enjoyment and relaxation and signifies the dedication and care invested in creating a safe and clean space for family and friends.

7. The knowledge and skills acquired through understanding pool maintenance can empower pool owners to tackle any challenge and maintain their pool in top condition.

8. Embracing the joy of a well-maintained pool is a rewarding endeavor that enriches the lives of pool owners and their loved ones, promoting a happier, healthier and more enjoyable future.

How often should I test my pool water, and what should I test for?

It is recommended to test your pool water at least once a week, and more frequently if the pool is being used heavily. You should test for pH, chlorine, alkalinity, and calcium hardness.

How often should I clean my pool?

You should clean your pool regularly to keep it looking and functioning at its best. This includes skimming debris from the surface, cleaning the pool walls and floor, and cleaning the pool filter. The frequency of cleaning will depend on how often the pool is used and the surrounding environment but at least once a week is a good rule of thumb.

. . .

How often should I add chemicals to my pool?

Chemicals should be added to the pool on a regular basis to maintain proper water balance and sanitation. The frequency of adding chemicals will depend on the size of the pool, the level of usage, and the local climate. Follow the manufacturer's instructions carefully when adding chemicals.

How do I keep my pool safe?

Pool safety is essential, especially if you have children or pets. Install a fence around the pool area, ensure that the pool cover is secure, and never leave children unattended in or around the pool. It is also a good idea to learn CPR and keep a first aid kit nearby.

What is the ideal temperature for my pool?

The ideal temperature for a pool will depend on personal preference and the intended use of the pool. Most people prefer a temperature between 78-82°F (25-28°C) for recreational swimming. If the pool is primarily used for exercise or therapy, a higher temperature may be desired.

How much does it cost to maintain a pool?

The cost of pool maintenance will vary depending on factors such as the size of the pool, the type of pool, the frequency of use, and the local climate. On average, pool owners can expect to spend several hundred to several thousand dollars per year on maintenance costs.

How often should I backwash my pool filter?

The frequency of backwashing your pool filter will depend on the type of filter you have and the level of usage. Typically, sand filters should be backwashed every two to four weeks, while cartridge filters should be cleaned every two to three months.

How do I prevent algae growth in my pool?

Algae growth can be prevented by maintaining proper water chemistry, regular cleaning and maintenance, and using an algaecide when necessary. It is also important to remove debris and maintain proper circulation and filtration.

Can I swim in my pool while chemicals are being added?

It is generally safe to swim in your pool after adding chemicals, but it is recommended to wait until the chemical levels have been properly balanced and the water has been circulated for several hours.

What should I do if my pool water is cloudy?

Cloudy water can be a sign of imbalanced water chemistry, poor circulation, or other maintenance issues. Test the water chemistry and adjust as necessary, clean the pool filter, and improve circulation by running the pump and skimmer more frequently.

How long should I run my pool pump each day?

The length of time you should run your pool pump each day will depend on the size of your pool and the flow rate of your pump. In general, a pool pump should run for eight to twelve hours per day to maintain proper circulation and filtration.

Can I use a pool cover to reduce evaporation and heat loss?

Yes, using a pool cover is an effective way to reduce evaporation and heat loss from your pool. A cover can also help to keep debris out of your pool, reduce chemical use, and save energy costs.

How do I winterize my pool?

Winterizing your pool involves preparing it for the colder months when it will not be in use. This includes draining the pool to a safe level, adding winterizing chemicals, and covering the pool with a winter pool cover.

Can I use a robotic pool cleaner to clean my pool?

Yes, a robotic pool cleaner can be a convenient and efficient way to clean your pool. These cleaners are designed to scrub the pool walls and floor and remove debris, leaving your pool clean and clear. Be sure to follow the manufacturer's instructions carefully and clean the filter regularly.

How do I prevent and treat pool stains?

Pool stains can be caused by a variety of factors, such as metal content, organic material, and improper water balance. To prevent pool stains, maintain proper water chemistry, brush the pool regularly and add metal sequestering agents to the water. To treat pool stains, use specialized pool stain remover chemicals or consult with a professional for guidance.

How do I properly shock my pool?

Shocking your pool involves adding a high concentration of chlorine or other oxidizer to the water to kill bacteria and other contaminants. To properly shock your pool, follow the manufacturer's instructions carefully and ensure that the water chemistry is properly balanced beforehand. Also, wait to swim until the chlorine levels have returned to safe levels.

What should I do if I have a leak in my pool?

If you suspect a leak in your pool, it is important to identify the location and severity of the leak as soon as possible to prevent damage to the pool or surrounding area. You can perform a simple bucket test to determine if water is leaking from the pool. If you suspect a leak, contact a pool professional or the manufacturer for guidance.

How do I choose the right pool chemicals?

Choosing the right pool chemicals will depend on the specific needs of your pool and the water chemistry. It is important to use high-quality chemicals and follow the manufacturer's instructions carefully when adding chemicals to your pool. Consult with a professional if you are unsure which chemicals to use or how to use them properly.

What are the main chemicals I need?

There are several main chemicals you will need to properly maintain your pool's water chemistry. They are:

Chlorine

Chlorine is the most common pool sanitizer used to kill bacteria, viruses, and algae. It comes in various forms such as granular, liquid, and tablets.

pH Adjusters

pH adjusters, such as sodium carbonate and sodium bisulfate, are used to adjust the pH of the pool water to the recommended range of 7.2-7.8. Maintaining proper pH levels is important for water clarity, swimmer comfort, and to prevent equipment damage.

Alkalinity Adjusters

Alkalinity adjusters, such as sodium bicarbonate, are used to maintain the total alkalinity of the pool water within the recommended range of 80-120 parts per million (ppm). Proper alkalinity levels help to stabilize the pH and prevent rapid fluctuations.

Calcium Hardness Adjusters

Calcium hardness adjusters, such as calcium chloride, are used to maintain the proper level of calcium in the pool water, which helps to prevent corrosion and scale buildup in the pool and equipment.

Algaecides

Algaecides are used to prevent and treat algae growth in the pool water. There are several types of algaecides available, including copper-based, quaternary ammonium-based, and polyquat-based.

Shock

Shock is a high concentration of chlorine used to quickly kill bacteria and oxidize contaminants in the pool water. Shock should be used regularly to maintain proper sanitation and prevent algae growth.

It is important to use high-quality chemicals and follow the manufacturer's instructions carefully when adding chemicals to your pool. You should also regularly test your pool water to ensure proper chemical balance and adjust chemical levels as necessary. If you are unsure about which chemicals to use or how to use them properly, consult with a professional or the manufacturer for guidance.

Thank you for your time!

If this book has brought you enjoyment and enriched your knowledge, I would greatly appreciate it if you could take a moment to leave a review. Your feedback not only helps me, but also other pool owners who can benefit from the valuable insights contained within these pages. Please leave a review where ever you purchased this book. Thank you for your support and for helping to spread the word about this book.

Made in the USA
Coppell, TX
06 September 2023

21292453R00074